THE CONFIDENCE CHASM

Joe D. Batten
Gail Batten

 American Management Association

© *American Management Association, Inc., New York, 1972.*
All rights reserved. Printed in the United States of America.

This publication may not be reproduced, stored in a retrieval system,
or transmitted in whole or in part, in any form or by any means,
electronic, mechanical, photocopying, recording, or otherwise,
without the prior written permission of the Association.

International standard book number: 0–8144–5309–0
Library of Congress catalog card number: 72–82875

First printing

Foreword

*Do we desperately try to "rap"? Have
"dialogue"? Do our arms and minds
falter as we attempt to reach one another
across the void of the years? Do we
continue to defer to weaknesses in order
to mask our own?*

or:

*Do we confidently begin to fill—and to
close—the chasm opened by anxieties,
retreat, and invective that can have no
place in the world of today and
tomorrow? Do we truly come together
in mutually supportive confidence?*

For years it has been an axiom that people become what
they think. That groups, cultures, and societies are indeed
products of their individual and collective thoughts. It is
a major premise or hypothesis of this book that to a lesser
extent, but in a very real way, people *become what they
say.* We are told there is a communication gap—one
amounting to a veritable chasm—between the generations
and that it may be unbridgeable because of "differing sets
of values." It is a further premise of this book that these

value systems are relatively similar but only *seem* vastly different owing to erroneous interpretations of the values of others based on certain superficial observations. In short, the chasm—however wide and deep—*can* be bridged. What plagues us is a *confidence* chasm.

In support of these two hypotheses, we are going to roam far beyond the stereotypes of today's mass communications media and look in on the young and the old (or older) in a variety of ways, times, and places. Our remarks are intended for all those who lead and shape—or will lead and shape—the direction of the institutions that make up our society. In those instances where a particularly stinging remark is made, we'd like it understood that in virtually every case one of the authors is speaking about his/her own peer group.

The confidence chasm is implicit in the whole milieu of our society. Yet it is an imprecise thing. So we have sought—and are seeking—a new form of precision. That is, we are trying to find the precise ideas necessary and central to a new, vigorous society—a society which can actualize the beautiful, noble, and ever joyful precepts upon which it was founded. May—and we hope this rather fervently—the resulting book be shot through with realistic prospects and paths for tomorrow.

The Authors

Contents

1

Dialogue of Doom

MEN grow when inspired by a high purpose, when contemplating horizons," said Alex Carrel. "The sacrifice of oneself is not very difficult for one burning with the passion for a great adventure."

So where do we find our great adventure these days? Where do we start? What are we saying to one another about the world in which we live and the future that lies ahead for us?

First, it might perhaps be well to consider, rather, what we should *quit* saying. This is the statement, so often heard, that everything is bound to go wrong; that there is something basically bad about all human beings and that all human history is evil, irrational, without purpose. When we begin to talk this way, and when we begin to think this way, we begin to *become* this way. And when you have people—in large groups as nations or in small groups as departments or divisions or families—beginning to interact with each other on the basis of gloomy, cynical, or even despairing expectations, almost always those expectations will be borne out.

On a deeper level—and at one extreme of the spectrum —is the impact of invective and obscenity on our organizations, our people, our very way of life. James Michener's *Kent State: What Happened and Why* provides some grim, compelling, tough-minded challenges. For instance:

> The debasement of language is one of the most powerful agencies for the destruction of existing society. . . . The assault on language is the spearhead of an assault on all authority.[1]

And Dr. S. I. Hayakawa says in a mind-stretching column:

> Words are rarely "mere." Courteous and reasonable words, addressed even to those with whom we are in sharp disagreement, are invitations to discourse and debate. They are an acknowledgment of the other fellow's basic humanity. Obscenities, on the other hand, unless spoken in jest, are a studied rejection of the other fellow's basic humanity.[2]

Take the American manager (and we include here those who manage virtually all kinds of organizations and groups). As an individual, he—and sometimes she—has demonstrated abilities entrepreneurially and otherwise which have literally startled and thrilled the world. Certainly he has played a unique role in the development of the United States of America. His capacity for getting results has been proved time and again.

Yet this capacity and those results have lately been obscured by abuse heaped especially on the U.S. businessman, a contemptuous evaluation of his ethics (or lack of ethics) and the climate in which he operates. This judgment originated with those who have announced loudly their determination never to compromise their personal values and become "part of the system," and by now it is credited so universally as almost to pass for fact. As a consequence, the businessman himself is beginning to believe what he hears from all sides—and the capacity and the results are being threatened accordingly.

This book is in many ways a call to leaders of all ages and kinds, managers in business and industry included, to appraise the past and present dispassionately; to respond objectively to the challenge of criticism and set new targets for themselves; to undertake the stretching quest for greater understanding of human beings and human events. Surely this will be the stuff of management as we surge into the seventies.

O.K., So What?

Maybe, we concede, maybe. But then what do we hear ourselves saying?

"This world is a son-of-a-bitch—I guess that's why I stay a perpetual student. I don't have to face everybody outside." Here we have a statement by a 19-year-old university youth who is barely on the verge of his life. It is a typical lament from today's turned-off generation.

Wholesale admiration of writers who dwell on expedients and cop-outs is a common fault nowadays—in too many of us. In those who are older and should know better, it grows out of the desire to be thought sophisticated, "with it." In too many young people, it saps initiative; it traps boys and girls in coffeehouses where one gloomy thought leads to another until the very mind begins to clog in the smoky atmosphere. *This is where it's supposed to be at.* And that's where it will have to start if we are to feel true love and empathy, real warmth and sympathy for one another; if minds are to be unclogged and freed from put-downs and negatives that leave no room for understanding.

In so many ways we become liberated or trapped—committed or turned off—by the words we hear and the words we learn to use, which in turn become the foundation for our attitudes and the concepts and objectives that will guide us throughout our entire lives. To get meaningful results, we must conceive, and be dedicated to, meaningful goals.

That Society Is Great Wherein . . .

More than 30 years ago Alfred North Whitehead, the great Harvard sage, declared: "That society is great wherein its men of business think greatly of their functions."

Professor Whitehead was ahead of his time, but at least we are beginning to see evidence of a new kind of thinking on the part of the businessman. Indeed, his concern about society as a whole, and about the problems and needs of the many varied segments of our population, has become one of the major stories in the ongoing saga of business in America. But the usual interpretation of Whitehead's statement—to the effect that he was simply urging more involvement in society—does not cut deeply enough. He may have meant (as increasing numbers of us now believe) that it is vital for the manager to see his function as presently or potentially *good, significant, relevant*—as fundamental to the requirements of an actualized society. When the man of business or the manager in any type of human endeavor denigrates and/or doubts the worth, rightness, and significance of his function, he diminishes his capacity to do great and good things in, through, and with that function.

No Need for Obsolescence

Of course, it takes mental and moral muscle to deliberately set out to *increase* one's capacity to do good and great things. Many men and women never make the effort, much less see the necessity for it, yet to do otherwise is to become obsolete.

Bert Farquhar, the stereotype of a middle manager, is a case in point. Forty-two years old, he has gradually been becoming obsolete for half of that time. At first glance he might have stepped right out of the pages of a Horatio Alger book. Certainly his material wealth has increased beyond his most extravagant expectations—but in direct proportion to the decline of his physical, mental, and spiritual riches. Unfortunately, he has come to accept the cheap, cynical, materialistic attitudes which we hear expressed over and over in today's world. He has become what he thinks and says, in other words. He has diminished, not increased, his capacity to do great and good things.

Yet Bert Farquhar doesn't need to remain obsolete! If a person is indeed the product of what he thinks and says, there are means that can be explored, changes that can be made, to free up new viability and relevance.

The Effrontery of Despair:
Who Do You Think You Are?

There is a present-day phenomenon (Bert Farquhar is a victim of it) that we might call the "effrontery of despair." As an illustration, let's take the case of the administrative engineer who said: "No matter how carefully I seem to plan for developing a new product modification or selling a new process or getting budgetary approval for a new project, somebody always seems to be conspiring to make sure I don't succeed. I often think that life itself may be one great big conspiracy to keep me from accomplishing what I would like to accomplish."

The question asked of this man, in a private counseling session, was: "Who do you think you are? What makes you think other people consider you important enough to spend their time plotting and scheming and dreaming up ways to thwart you?" What he was doing in reality was simply grasping at an expedient, trying to escape from having to confront on-the-job difficulties that he might have turned into challenges.

In much the same vein a coed said: "There are so many things I want to talk about with people, but I can't. You know why? People are rotten. Oh, a few can be trusted, but not many. I just don't dare take the risk." In short, a 20-year-old girl had—she thought—the wisdom to judge and put down thousands of human beings as a result of her daily conversations with other students. A few disillusioning experiences and she was ready to doubt everybody.

Unfortunately, this girl was not atypical. She, like many other adults and young people, had built herself a protective shield of aloofness and exclusivity; she felt people were constantly trying to battle down her defenses and move in on her. It's a kind of far-out ego trip to imagine that you are so important to others and to judge and hate entire groups of people on this basis.

Parents vs. Children vs. Precedent

When you come right down to it, blanket dismissal of the older generation by the other, or vice versa, is senseless. More than that, it is a tragic waste. Some time ago, on Youth Sunday at a large metropolitan church, a group of parents and teenagers met for "dialogue" after the regular service. It was interesting and all too familiar to note that the blackboard had been divided into two sections. One was headed: "What's wrong with teenagers?" The other: "What's wrong with parents?" And the discussion, the resulting trips to the microphone on the part of each age group, added up predictably to one more session of diatribe, finger pointing, and the big put-down. This had been going on for about an hour when, suddenly, one of the young people—a girl—walked up to the microphone and announced: "I'm going to talk to my own peer group now. I'd like you parents just to sit there and say nothing for a while."

First of all, she wrote on the blackboard, "What's *right* with parents?" Then she began to tell the other members of her young peer group how she saw the older generation. She challenged the group to acknowledge that parents had problems (some of which the younger generation had contributed to); that they gave much to their children; and that, perhaps, their seeming lack of understanding and concern was often simply an inadequacy in the vocabularies

7

of both parties and in their power to communicate. Finally, and without warning, she said: "Now I want to hand the microphone to my dad. He'll talk to your parents."

In his turn, the father challenged his fellow parents to look for things that were *right* with their kids and to try to build on these positives. "A weakness," he said, "is the absence of a strength," and he went on to ask, "Why build on minuses when pluses are all that we really can depend on in our relations with each other?" Nothing can be *built* with zeros, vacuums, minuses, or "absences." And that's precisely what weaknesses are.

Precedent has always said (so far) that youth is bound to cause trouble, but that the trouble will pass and the whole bunch will soon begin to marry, have children, and realize that maybe the Old Man was smarter than they thought. But it needn't always be parents vs. children vs. precedent. It can just as logically, and perhaps more logically, be parents *plus* children *plus* precedent.

The Easy Thing Is the Expedient Thing

Strengths, we have said, are the only real building material, the only real mortar for effective human relationships. Why, then, not vastly accelerate the search for these strengths? Because it requires guts and because the time-worn preoccupation with weaknesses is so easy, so tempting, and so familiar. It is the *expedient* thing. Too often, the will and energy needed to focus on strengths rather than weaknesses are missing—on both sides of the generation gap.

Somehow, in the classrooms, dormitories, and public

parks of the seventies—the places where modern youth gathers—an outlook appears to be all too prevalent which will not, cannot, restore the ready communication with their adult "friends" that so many young people have lost. Why? In part, at least, because hard work—physical and mental—has become relatively unknown in American universities. (And, it must be conceded, the aversion against any kind of effort is shared by many adults.) One needs only to look around at the sagging shoulders, pudgy bellies, waddling gait, and lackluster eyes to realize that physical activity frequently is nonexistent. The vitality necessary for a questing mind is too often dissipated in unaired dormitory rooms and nightly "keggers."

Likewise, an active body adds muscle—pure protein, not fatty tissue. And, like an active body, a vigorous, questing mind enjoys moving quickly from subject to subject. Perhaps the main problem is simply that "fatty" brain cells are no substitute for the real gray matter and thoughts are jumbled and uncoordinated. Wouldn't it be better to have mental *muscles* rather than mental misery? Then it would be easy to look for strengths instead of weaknesses. If, that is, it weren't for still another obstacle in the way: distrust.

Distrust is a classic manifestation of the psychological defense mechanism known as *projection*. We can't trust others if we don't trust ourselves. We can't trust ourselves if we overemphasize, or dwell on, our own weaknesses.

It seems so much easier to opt for the expedient thing. Meanwhile, precious little thought is devoted to strengths and far too much to weaknesses. Nor have we yet developed the vocabulary we need to focus on strengths in, for example, performance appraisal and career counseling.

You Get What You Give

The term "servomechanism" has been defined in many ways. Webster calls it "an automatic device for controlling large amounts of power by means of very small amounts of power and automatically correcting performance of a mechanism." Thus a flow of energy returns to the source of its original impulse and—through the closed loop—renews itself constantly, so that it constitutes a form of perpetual motion. It maintains an ongoing, continuous force and relies on the physical fact that for every action there should, and can, be a reaction.

A cybernetic unit (the word stems from the Greek *cyber* or *kyber,* meaning "steersman") is a sophisticated version of a servomechanism; that is, it possesses a *built-in* corrective guidance system. Here in this book we shall proceed from the premise that human beings are by far the most splendid cybernetic units of all. Therefore, if optimum effectiveness is to be achieved, the fuel for these cybernetic units—the value system of the individual mind—must be stocked with cybernetic values.

A cogent summary of cybernetic truth is implicit in Galatians 6:7: "Whatsoever a man soweth, that shall he reap." In more colloquial words, "You get what you give."

Some of the new jargon one hears today (and we don't mean this derogatorily) can and does evoke a variety of emotions in the generations. Think of terms like "delphi exercises," "synergistic symbiosis," "T-groups," "lateral thinking," "synectics," "Electric Kool-Aid Acid Test." They can repel or impel, attract or reject, turn on or turn off. It all depends, as it should, on the individual. We submit at this preliminary stage that virtually all these

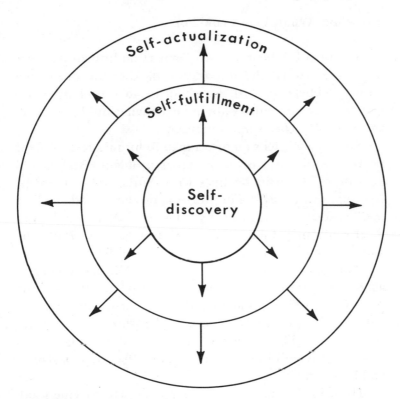

terms and the techniques they identify are fundamentally concerned with three things—and they are really indivisible: self-actualization, self-fulfillment, self-discovery.

Jargon or not, the sort of language we are talking about represents approaches to knowledge of self that are promising. We hope that those concerned will not be stultified by overly academic and scientistic verbosity but will increasingly discover clean, lean, crisp, forceful words to use without apology in the quest for individual and organizational purpose, direction, and significance.

You Find What You Look For

Socrates of Athens, an early expert on human development, understood the importance of knowing one's own nature. "The man with full knowledge would never do evil because the fully enlightened man would recognize the damaging effects upon himself."

For instance, let's picture a man in his mid-forties. Bent nearly double because of a spinal problem. Gray-haired because of the pain he lives with. Surely he is more or less qualified to say, "The world is no darn good—look at *me!*" Instead, when asked by a friend, "What would you do if confronted by the author of *The Passover Plot?*" he says, "I would defeat him with love." And he would.

This man is not looking for gloom. He has plenty of agony every minute. He lives each day looking for the beauty and warmth and love that are innate in man and nature. He will find it because he thinks and craves nothing else. The particular man we're discussing has, in fact, recently published a book entitled *This Joy of Mine—* and he *means* it!

He brings to mind a younger man—an extremely talented artist who can capture the vitality of a snorting horse or the guileless simplicity of a puppy. Working all his life with only one eye, he has put great strain on his vision. While talking about his passion for creating beautiful things, he once said: "You know, I just can't read trash any more or go to X-rated movies. It fills my mind with ugliness, and that stops up the good which flows through my brushes. With all earth's beauty, why fill my mind with unnecessary filth?"

This young man hasn't had it easy. He grew up in a slum and lost his eye in a knife fight, which might have given him an easy excuse for cynicism. Be he loved the beauty of a vibrant, breathing animal and dedicated his life to reproducing it.

Would it be safe, then, to say this? That "society is great wherein people have a genuine zest for living each day and for every moment trying to replace a put-down with a build-up." Perhaps the very notion of building instead of destroying frightens many because destruction has become the basis for their existence.

Language That Turns People On

What the current crop of doomsayers don't seem to realize—at least never mention—is that American history has been a constant ebb and flow of protest leading to periodic crises of authority. These crises, which can be shown quite readily on a graph, have generally been led by the intellectuals, with students performing as the foot soldiers and mouthing words that reflect despair, anger, and preoccupation with evil and human weakness. We're advancing the idea here that it takes courage to use, instead, language that has some sparkle, some glow, and some strength.

Why the retreat from words which smack of power and purpose? Why this fear of strength? Walter Lippmann knew better. More than 20 years ago he wrote:

> The revelation has been made. By it man conquered the jungle about him and the *barbarian within him.* [Italics ours.] The elementary principles of work and sacrifice and duty—and the transcendent criteria of truth, justice and righteousness and the grace of love and charity—are the things which have made men free.[3]

These are words which can move men's souls and stir them to action. To repeat: We not only become what we *think,* we become what we *say.* Yet we still hear the comment (which would be amusing if it were not so tragic) made so often in potentially catalytic meetings across the country: "Don't let's deal in semantics and rhetoric—we must do something practical."

Here, however, is the manifest fact: It is essential for ideals to be *articulated* before objectives can be set and action organized, targeted, monitored, and accomplished. Thus in the age of the mind, in the age of what we have called cybernetics, words have become in a very real sense potent instruments for social change; for change in business practices; for change in international affairs; for bridging what we have termed the confidence chasm.

The ability to articulate words is one of the principal factors distinguishing man from the lower forms of animal life. We etch out our dignity as individuals, our right to call ourselves human beings, in direct proportion to our ability to use words for constructive, stretching, humanity-perpetuating purposes. And now, over and over, we shrink from this kind of vocabulary. Over and over the dialogue of doom seems to offer the best sort of cop-out; it calls for avoiding words that cannot be ignored (*a la* Lippmann) and looks for dull, mundane, even obscene words which make it tolerable and comfortable for us to clot together in a state of rationalized torpor.

What's happened to *heroic* language? This is the kind that, a generation or two ago, turned young people on; it challenged them, it reached them, it stretched them. But perhaps the timeless verities of truth and justice, hard work, and, above all, the surmounting of difficulties—have lost their former appeal. Only temporarily, we hope. Perhaps they just sound a little bit too formidable for many people, young and old, in this country today.

Not "What's Wrong?" but "How Can It Be Made *Right?*"

It might be easy to conclude at this point that we are leveling our damning charges chiefly at the young. So let's switch scenes for a moment and take a look at the kind of conversation which has helped to create the climate and the pervasive, impressively intellectual, and all too ably articulated language of negativism and dissent.

Some time ago, the program director of a major television station in one of the country's largest metropolitan centers picked up his telephone. "Mr. Batten," he asked when the connection was made, "will you appear on one of our talk shows here? The moderator has a popular, although controversial, program; he really works visitors over. Are you willing to risk it?" "Yes," came the answer, "I'll take that chance."

As they sat waiting for the little red light on the camera to turn on, moderator and visitor cleared their throats, straightened their ties, combed their hair—in short, did the usual things. Suddenly it occurred to the visitor to ask, "Shouldn't we touch base before we go on camera? Isn't there something you would like to know about me or my thinking?" At that the moderator turned and with his assured manner, in his machined network-announcer tones, said, "The secret of this program's success is that everything is spontaneous. Nothing is rehearsed." "Thank you" was the only possible answer.

The little red light came on. The moderator leaned forward and said confidently and briskly, "Mr. Batten, will you tell us what is wrong with our nation?" "No!" said the visitor. What were actually seconds probably seemed like minutes to the moderator; his aplomb seemed to dwindle. At last he said, "I simply can't understand this, Mr. Batten. I understand that you have written a number of books and that you believe in speaking out on these matters, that you believe much change must take place. Yet you won't answer my question."

"What's your question again?" the visitor countered. "What's wrong with our nation?" the moderator repeated, and this time got his answer. "No, I won't answer that because millions of people seem to be addressing themselves to it. On the contrary, if you'd like me to speak about what ought to be done to make things more *right* with our nation, if you'd like to talk about some of our present, latent, and potential *strengths,* then I'll be happy to discuss them with you."

The moderator looked relieved, the two began to talk, and what was going to be a 10-minute interview turned into a 30-minute one. At the end of the program, the switchboard was glutted with calls, virtually all of them highly affirmative and enthusiastic—indicating, in effect, that the viewers' hope for the future of our country had been reinforced. We submit that in our land there is a great *hunger*—although still only a faltering quest—for joy and affirmation.

What's the point here? It is this: Those few allotted minutes might have added to the ballast, the almost contrived legacy of despair and confusion about the future which a good many viewers undoubtedly were feeling. Some of them might even, perhaps, have been encouraged to make the decision to "drop out" in one way or another. And dropping out, as we know, can take the form of suicide, abandoning a family, electing the alcohol or drug route to hell, or adopting other, less extreme forms of backing away from the confrontations which are so necessary to all of us.

Something Bigger to Live For

I wonder how many people have reflected on the aftermath of—or the subsequent attitudes induced by—some of the "misery loves company" conversations that we so often hear at social gatherings, at staff meetings, at the dinner table, in airports, or you name it.

What we are saying here, at the start of this book, is that words can encourage a set of individual and collective attitudes that add up to total indifference, inertia, repression, depression—call it what you will. The power of words is potent to the point of utter destruction, all the more so because it remains largely unstudied in terms of its ultimate potential. For instance, what about the net contribution of Alvin Toffler's words in the closing pages of his massive and much discussed book, *Future Shock:*

> Our first and most pressing need, therefore, before we can begin to gently guide our evolutionary destiny, before we can build a humane future, is to halt the runaway acceleration that is subjecting multitudes to the threat of future shock while, at the same moment, intensifying all the problems they must deal with—war, ecological incursions, racism, the obscene contrast between rich and poor, the revolt of the young, and the rise of a potentially deadly mass irrationalism.

17

There is no facile way to treat this wild growth, this cancer in history. There is no magic medicine, either, for curing the unprecedented disease it bears in its rushing wake: future shock. I have suggested palliatives for the change-pressed individual and more radically curative procedures for the society—new social services, a future-facing education system, new ways to regulate technology, and a strategy for capturing control of change. Other ways must also be found. Yet the basic thrust of this book is diagnosis. For diagnosis precedes cure, and we cannot begin to help ourselves until we become sensitively conscious of the problem.

These pages will have served their purpose if, in some measure, they help create the consciousness needed for man to undertake the control of change, the guidance of his evolution. For, by making imaginative use of change to channel change, we can not only spare ourselves the trauma of future shock, we can reach out and humanize distant tomorrows.[4]

Here we find no words to stir the blood, to stimulate constructive action, to inaugurate viable improvement. Rather, the author seems to be sketching out a future that seems devoid of both hope and specific curative prescriptions. He says, ". . . the basic thrust of this book is diagnosis." But will not a steadily welling stream of grim "diagnosis" tend to inhibit creative change? Does any mature, responsible person need reminders of what's *wrong*—and the invariably morose dialogue that rolls out so easily? Most of us can quote yards of such discouraging diatribe and cite chapter and verse for it.

The chief executive of a major footwear-manufacturing company said of *Future Shock,* "When I read the book, I skipped the chapter on 'Social Futurism.' I was in a cold sweat—it scared the hell out of me." "What are you going to do about it?" he was asked. "Nothing," he said. "This book makes it clear that the odds are stacked against us."

But wait! Let's back up and read a portion of that chapter:

> Imagine the historic drama, the power and evolutionary impact, if each of the high-technology nations literally set aside the next five years as a period of national self-appraisal; if at the end of five years it were to come forward with its own tentative agenda for the future, a program embracing not merely economic targets but, equally important, broad sets of social goals—if each nation, in effect, stated to the world what it wished to accomplish for its people and mankind in general during the remaining 'quarter century of the millennium.[5]

How do you feel now? The fact is that deep in every normal person, whether young or old, whether manager or worker, is a need to think about, talk about, commit oneself to, and *live for* something bigger than self.

Herman Kahn, director of the Hudson Institute, told a recent meeting of top corporation executives—as reported in *The Washington Post*—that the biggest problem facing mankind is religious, the quest for meaning and purpose. "Why do we stay alive?" he asked. "What are we here for?" And he added: "My grandfather walked with God and knew why."

A Pattern for Change

As a society, we must

1. Determine the impact of positive versus negative semantics on a culture, society, or group.
2. Initiate a fundamental reorganization of educational institutions at all levels to implement our findings.
3. Note well the words of Theodore Roosevelt:

It is not the critic who counts, nor the man who points out how the strong man stumbles, or where the doer of deeds could have done better. The credit belongs to the man who is actually in the arena; whose face is marred by dust and sweat; who strives valiantly, who errs and may fail again, because there is no effort without error or shortcoming, but who does actually strive to do deeds; who does know the great enthusiasm, the great devotion; who spends himself in a worthy cause; who at the best, knows in the end the triumph of high achievement, and who at the worst, if he fails, at least fails while daring greatly, so that his place shall never be with those cold and timid souls who know neither victory nor defeat.

As individuals, we must

1. Carefully assess our own word arsenal and chart a program of vocabulary development, possibly using an easy-to-carry notebook. Add just one crisp, simple, powerful *new* word to our vocabulary each day.
2. Decide what we, personally, are going to do next . . .

REFERENCES

1. James Michener, *Kent State: What Happened and Why* (New York: Random House, 1971).
2. S. I. Hayakawa, "The Uses of Obscenity," *Des Moines Register,* August 15, 1971.
3. Walter Lippmann, *The New York Times,* June 6, 1971.
4. Alvin Toffler, *Future Shock* (New York: Random House, 1970), p. 486.
5. Ibid., p. 478.

2

Renewers or Renegers?

Of course, semantics—words—are by no means the only factors today that are having a divisive, destructive effect on human relationships and deepening the chasm between the generations. There is also the problem that members of either group, in judging the other, appear so often to think only in terms of superficialities. We hear a great deal from both sides about "affectations" and—more seriously—about "double standards" and apparent aimlessness and lack of goals.

Take, for instance, this matter of double standards. The seeming existence of such standards among the young people on our campuses and those under 26 or so in business or other organizational employment tends to vex the "mature" generation of, say, 35 and older. These are the same critics who refer endlessly to the affectations of the younger group. They can't see beyond the sometimes bizarre clothing, the casual manners, and what almost amounts—in their eyes—to a complete disregard for personal grooming. Yet they themselves occasion at least an equal amount of finger pointing, vexation, and frustration on the part of the young people they criticize so severely.

It's easy to say, "All right—you win," or, "I just can't make you see," and just walk away. It takes time to build a foundation for anything successful. And a quality life takes much more time and work to find. All the same, a steady, systematic refining and building of values eliminates the need to destroy. Thus in "doing your thing" the productive, rather than the expedient, becomes "the thing" to do.

The Affected Generation (Whose?)

Many a so-called mature business manager will insist that his principal objection to what he calls a "fine young group" in his organization is simply its "affectations." When asked what he means, he points to the hairdos, the sideburns, the mustaches, the "mod" fashions, and all the rest of it. Nor is he alone in his prejudice. Among older people in general, a great deal of resentment and, sometimes, veiled contempt and even a little sublimated fear seem to settle around such manifestations of the youth culture.

But is there really only one "affected" generation? Many young people, when asked what their principal objection is to the mature group, reply more or less like this: "Our parents and their peers are by and large practicing double standards. Sure, we know they have worked hard and done much to produce a better world in terms of material wealth. It's their phoniness, their affectations, those double standards that we object to."

Queried further, young people claim the "follow the crowd" syndrome is even stronger among the mature group than among themselves. They declare, for instance, that the parent generation pushes for the Cadillac, the boat, the country club (with, of course, just the right name), the golfing cart, the secretary, the office furniture, the carpet, the name on the door. They cite the "cocktail patois," the "right" church membership, the endless attention to the proper attire, and many other matters to which they seem to feel their elders have attached undue importance.

They point out, for instance, that in spite of these superficial signs of success, achievement, and solid citizenship, there is concrete evidence of the negative attitudes, values, and practices that they believe are exemplified in the lives of older people. They say that too many business executives have a tendency to rationalize "survival in the business jungle" tactics. They note the "frozen faces" and "frozen rage," the clear lack of real fulfillment. They wonder what's wrong with smoking pot when, as they say, the older generation's evening gaiety begins in a glass and ends in stupidity or grief or remorse. Why, they ask, should young people follow this example or in any way respect this pragmatic demonstration of the breakdown or at least the faulty practice of traditional American values?

Cooperative Listening

A young girl was seriously interested in competitive diving and swimming. Through constant practice and self-discipline, she had become one of the best in her field. When she began to learn in junior high school, her father had given her both encouragement and financial support.

He could not understand her enthusiasm at all, but he loved her and wanted her to be happy. He even listened and talked with her about the various routines she must perform and the dives she needed to learn.

During practice, the girl was often injured; she dove wrong or got bad fatigue cramps. But always Dad (though he wished she'd stop because he was afraid she might drown from exhaustion some night) smiled and listened as she rattled on. Eventually he became eager to help her and started to read about various aspects of swimming and diving. He became knowledgeable enough to watch and give constructive criticism which finally put the girl in a position to try out for the Olympic team.

By this time, Father was so interested that he wanted to learn diving himself. He asked his daughter to teach him. It was an unusual situation, but he knew this 20-year-old had both skill and a vast amount of practical experience. Tensions arose at first because the daughter approached Father as a student (she also had been teaching others), not as a parent. This put Dad on the defensive. But instead of yelling and demanding, the girl kept quiet; she didn't give her pupil orders but offered suggestions, and in this way she taught him successfully. He can now dive fairly well, and the father-daughter friendship has been strengthened.

Perhaps what happened here should be happening in all family relationships and in all families: *Cooperative listening occurred.* The daughter realized she needed someone to watch and criticize her and accepted the fact that although, to begin with, her father could not dive himself, he knew what she must do to improve. Most important, Dad did not feel obligated to play the role of heavy father and dictate to her. In the end, he asked her for help and so accepted the fact that his daughter could be an expert at something with which he had little practical experience.

Bridge—Or Chasm?

It might be said that at present there are two major kinds of reaction to the younger generation. The first, confident and cool, is typified by the swimmer's dad. The second is radical and critical, as demonstrated by the relationship of two brothers, 19 and 21, with their father. Jack, the younger brother, followed the yippie philosophy as he hitched around the country with his hair down to his shoulders: "Regardless of the issue—Bangladesh, lower pay for cops, blue skies, higher taxes—if you're sitting in and disrupting, I'll be there." Ted, a crisply dressed college student, spent all his free time doing volunteer counseling at a nearby church.

Each boy felt keenly about the disadvantaged people around him—the economic or racial discrimination they were subjected to—but each looked at social problems from a different vantage point. Ted saw life critically but tried to improve conditions insofar as he was able. Jack condemned the society that forced some people into poverty or discriminated against others because of their skin color, but this put-down was as far as he personally went. The trouble at home started when the boys' father began to feel inadequate in his peer group. A relatively successful salesman, he had long felt too smart for his job; and Ted, whom others admired enormously, irritated the older man no less than his nonconformist brother by being so enthusiastic about his counseling activities. When people commented on the two boys, the father would dismiss their remarks offhandedly: "Oh, Jack doesn't know *what* he's doing except grow hair, and Ted has his damn religion." As a consequence, neither boy felt able to communicate with his father, though they freely admitted they had real affection for him. Tension continued until Jack took off without a word on a cross-country journey "to find out about *it*"—whatever IT is!—and his father was left to wonder and worry.

Similar situations and families, but what a difference! Why the chasm in the one and a bridge in the other? Confidence—or the lack of it! With adequate confidence one can *listen* and *relate*. Without it personal relationships all too often resemble a house of cards.

Both these fathers, of approximately the same age and educational background, were the catalyst for understanding or misunderstanding within the family. Like the young swimmer, Ted was confident, bright, and successful; he might have established strong communication links with his father. Instead, he resolutely ignored his father's snide cracks about religion—a mind shield, created solely because of the put-downs aimed at him daily—which was as effective as Jack's affectation of indifference in killing off communication with the father. Only the swimmer cared enough to analyze the situation that had developed between her and her father—and had the guts to do something about it. Daughter, like father, had an unspoken goal she was determined, deep within herself, to accomplish. Thus each had enough confidence to admit he could use some help. Most important, the father was able to face the knowledge that his child could and did excel him in a sport!

The girl and her father were the *renewers*. They talked over the negative elements in their relationship and said unhesitatingly, "We'll try to correct them." Then they dwelt on their strengths and on ways to develop these that would replace the weaknesses. In contrast, the *renegers*—Ted and Jack and their father—lacked self-esteem. They were unable to accept one another as they were, and even felt obliged to turn away a genuine compliment directed at any of the three. Each was afraid that he himself deserved no praise; therefore, if he praised one of the others or listened while somebody else did so, he would receive no commendation in return. Lack of confidence can beget fear. Fear usually begets hate. Hate destroys confidence. And then the circle closes.

Goals and Dreams

The girl diver, we have pointed out, had a goal. So did her dad. This gave them not only self-confidence but the courage to reach across the threatening gap and establish real communication with one another. Ted also had goals in that he saw the problems of the numerous disadvantaged groups in our society and proposed to do whatever might be in his power to remedy them. His brother Jack saw the problems but chose to stand back and do nothing; he drifted along aimlessly and, in the end, copped out. As for the father of the boys, it had been so long since his life had had any purpose that he would have been nonplussed at the very notion of personal goal setting.

The girl diver obviously dreamed too. A dream can become a goal if it has sufficient focus; the trouble is, it may trail off into idle, unformed hopes and wishful thinking without *the nourishment called confidence*. And, at this point, any chance to turn it into an actual, conscious goal capable of achievement will have been lost.

"What needs to be done to these college students right now is to yank away their money supply and force them to work their way through school for at least a year." No, this statement comes not from the older side but from a 20-year-old university student with very definite goals and the determination and confidence to achieve them. Totally self-supporting while he works his way through flight training, this young man attends class from 8:00 A.M. to 2:00 P.M., flies airplanes until 4:00 P.M., and is on the job from 9:00 P.M. to 3:00 A.M. Upon graduation, he'll know he has earned whatever success he achieves alone—with parental encouragement, to be sure, but entirely by his own efforts.

Clearly this young man's goals for the future have to do with more than just finishing school and getting a good job. Though busy, he is intensely interested in people, ideas, and solutions to the various problems that seem to beset campus life. He spends little time on sit-ins and protests, but he is devoting much time and effort to earning and to acquiring abilities which eventually will enable him to help the causes which concern him. He is therefore qualified—if anyone is—to indict his fellow students.

The conglomerate affectations of both groups—young people and adults—show strongly that not enough dreaming, mind stretching, and goal setting take place. In young people, as a result, the search for significance may take the form of overly luxuriant hair, wild clothing, and a generally uninviting appearance. Their disillusioned, harried elders may console themselves for the emptiness of their lives with alcohol, gambling, illicit sex, whatever. In both cases there is too eager agreement with those most agreed with, too little dreaming (or too much unfocused daydreaming), and a lot of talk about goals without ever setting any.

A dream or a goal, in the last analysis, cannot be realized without a system of principles. Then the habit of setting and achieving realistic yet progressively more difficult goals must be established: Dream an easy-to-reach goal, reach it, dream again—and this time be a little more ambitious. Now a foundation has been started which can be built upon.

Needing to feel "with it" or "cool" becomes less and less important as dreams and visions are fulfilled.

Who Cares?

Recently, in a residential area of a large American city, four horses—ridden by two teenage girls each—occupied the full width of the street. Numerous cars driven by adults carefully swung out around or wove with seemingly infinite patience through the young riders. In passing, the drivers registered varying degrees of anger, annoyance, or frustration that were mirrored in their faces as they speeded up again and went on.

Eventually, a man approaching in his car on his own side of the street asked the girls to move over. Full of themselves as teenagers often are, not caring or perhaps secretly elated that they were managing to inconvenience great numbers of adults, they challenged him laughingly. "Go around us!" they chorused. "Who do you think you are?"

The man stopped, got out of his car, and scolded the youthful riders briskly. In the process he explained why they were wrong to block traffic and what they *ought to do* instead. As he drove away, he appeared relaxed and happy. And—get this!—the riders looked as much stimulated as chastened. *Somebody had cared enough* about them to call them to task for their bad manners. Significantly, they stayed on the right side of the street from then on.

A Pattern for Change

It is high time we

1. Overhauled family-counseling services so as to eradicate the *roots* (crises of confidence) of conflict and promote true communication between the generations.
2. Significantly modified educational curricula and methods as well as the development programs established by business firms and other organizations so as to provide behavior-changing stimuli and build character. For example, meetings might be held during which each participant, young or old, would write out his answers to such questions as

    a. What is my most important goal?
    b. What is my biggest problem?
    c. What is one thing I am *for?*
    d. What is my greatest strength?

The replies could be compiled in some fashion and used as the raw material for unstructured but positive "encounter sessions" (in the best sense of that term) on a regular basis. Naturally, both discipline and diligence would have to be exercised in order to *build on strengths* and not dwell on weaknesses.

3

Expertise or Expedience?

Words—yes, words—can become exquisitely balanced "instruments" for clarifying goals, eliminating the superficial, and creating a life of dignity, worth, even beauty and nobility. Go back—if you care enough—and check out the root meaning of words in simple Latin and Greek texts prepared for just that purpose. You'll discover how watered down and dull-edged we've allowed many of these instruments to become. How about, instead, converting language from a series of crude bludgeons or, at best, blunt and ineffectual tools to a real means of therapy?

It's no easy thing to deliberately use words that are going to embarrass many of your contemporaries; to resist the popular, follow-the-leader attitude; to cultivate the habit of setting progressively tougher goals for yourself. Nobody ever said it was. How much simpler to say, when you miss out on something you wanted desperately, "Oh, I didn't really care all that much about it!" But then the dawn will rise on a discontented, not an actualized, individual.

Research, both modern and ancient, says clearly that difficulties—tough confrontations—are virtually essential to real success and self-actualization.

The Age-Old Accusation

The charge is often aimed at our young people that they never had it rough—that they don't know how to work and how to face up to difficult situations. This is nothing new. Parents have been complaining about children, managers about younger subordinates, drill sergeants about raw recruits, for as long as anyone can remember.

Such generalizations, however, can be dangerous. They ignore the fact that many older, supposedly mature men and women have chosen and continue to choose expedient patterns of work and life philosophies.

Lately we've been hearing all too many cheaply clever statements like this: "In a hierarchy each individual tends to rise to his level of incompetence." There is, of course, a kind of truth in this so-called principle—unfortunately. But how numbed and expediency-prone can we get? How silly and feeble? The bald fact of the matter is that, relatively speaking, we still know virtually nothing of man's ultimate potential for growth, productivity, building, love, truth, joy, and wonder. We still, as a society, know so little about planned programs to develop—through planned difficulties—toughness of mind and spirit and emotional staying power.

The Findings of Dr. Link

Over 30 years ago, Dr. Henry Link graduated from one of our major universities as an honor student with a Ph.D. in psychology. As he puts it in his book, for the next several years he lived a life of adequacy; a life of reasonable satisfaction. He became a member of the faculty of another university and began to practice psychological consulting privately. Then he received a large sum from a foundation. His targeted objectives? To determine the common denominators in the lives of people throughout the United States which contributed to a state of happiness. Dr. Link put together a sound, professional group of researchers who spread out across the country to determine what a cross-section of Americans of all types, at all levels of our society, could tell them about the requirements for a life of fulfillment and effectiveness.

After several years, Dr. Link's carefully collated and assessed results yielded several very interesting findings. He found, among other things, that one of the most important ingredients in the life of a happy person is that virtually every day, after he reaches a certain age of self-determination, it becomes important for him to do something *difficult;* something which makes him reach down within himself and find a new kind of strength, a new capacity for coping, new answers, new staying power.

On the other hand, Dr. Link found, a common denominator in the lives of most unhappy people is precisely the opposite. Over many years they have developed an expedient set of attitudes that may be virtually unconscious, even sublimated. And certainly they have acquired *an accompanying vocabulary that enables them to avoid doing anything that is very difficult.* Consequently, as the years go by, they build up a ballast or legacy of guilt which, in turn, contributes to feelings of inadequacy and self-loathing. And, as these feelings multiply, their willingness and ability to face difficult situations continue to dwindle accordingly. Thus a vicious circle is forged which becomes increasingly hard for such "unhappy" people to break out of.

The Protean Placebo (What?)

An executive from a large San Francisco corporation declares to anyone who will listen, "The universities are doing a lousy job—every damned one of them. All they are doing is training students to become radicals and drug addicts. Hell's fire! Just take a look at the speakers invited to speak on these campuses. And, boy, do they get some big fees for doing it!" When asked what he would do if *he* were invited to speak to a class or at a symposium, he says emphatically, "Not a chance! I'm no speaker—besides, they'd throw rocks at me!"

What an easy out! Here is an excellent example of how readily you can point one finger without realizing that when you do this there are three pointing back at you.

Many students, when queried about their reactions to speakers of various kinds on campus, mention that their principal objection to the average businessman or other representative of the "straight" portion of our sociey is that he seems to speak with diffidence, almost with apology, that he seems to be overly concerned about what the students may think of what he has to say. Questioned further about their reactions to some of the radical speakers they have heard, the students admit that although the content of the talk and even the appearance of the visitor, in numerous cases, weren't so great or the cause being promoted wasn't one they particularly identified with *initially,* they began to listen because the speaker appeared to be utterly sincere, deeply committed, and certainly not backward about advancing his viewpoint.

This sort of thing ought to be a source of great concern to the conscientious, public-spirited, dedicated business-man. Who has a better story to tell to young people than he? (If you doubt this, we invite you to visit your friendly librarian and review some facts.) The great practical achievements, the difficulties overcome, and, yes, the truly humanitarian accomplishments of the vast majority of men and women representing the economic sector of the American free enterprise system deserve a better "press" these days, on campus and elsewhere. They deserve journalists who have the courage and confidence to write it like it *really* is.

For the enlightenment of the "business apologist," we quote Thomas R. Shepard, Jr., publisher of the late lamented *Look*—in full confidence that such views as these had nothing to do with the magazine's recent demise.

> Environmentalists to the contrary, there is precisely as much oxygen in the air today as in 1910. Despite pollution, drinking water is safer than ever before, certainly safer than that which caused Philadelphia's 1793 epidemic which killed one of every five residents. If the present drop in U.S. birth rates continues, nobody will be here in the year 4000, but don't worry about that. Fish caught 44 years ago contained double the mercury of any fish processed this year. While 50 species of wildlife will probably become extinct in this century, the same number disappeared in the 1890s. Life expectancy of Americans has doubled in 150 years. DDT has

saved countless lives, though killing some birds and fish. Banning detergents might result in even worse ills. And our economic system, with all its faults, is the world's best.[1]

O.K., you purveyors of doomsday doctrines, what's your response? Our environment may be in greater danger than is implied here, but the record of U.S. business and industry is creditable—and of long standing. If you doubt Shepard's statement, so be it. But perhaps you'll undertake a little private research that will cause you to *doubt your doubts*—one of those difficult tasks that so many of us put off indefinitely (and that is one measure of a real intellectual).

A Pattern for Change

Qualified individuals and groups must further test Dr. Link's findings to determine whether the confrontation of difficulties does indeed build confidence and joy.

Perhaps the executive of the San Francisco corporation was telling us something he didn't quite realize. It takes a strong measure of real confidence in oneself to listen, to sit there with your guard down, let the other person in, and *let you out*. It requires a strong measure of personal security to be able not only to *listen* but to *hear*. You can't just sit and wonder, "What might he say that could in some way threaten me? How can I impress him by the way in which *I* say certain things? Impress him with my senior position? With my intellectual stature? With my all-round worthwhileness?" It's a pity that this executive doesn't like himself enough to listen, get the facts—then act. But he simply won't take the risk. You see, sudden insight into some hitherto unknown strengths just might pull or goad

him into some stretching and productive *actions*. And—
he'd have to get off his fat status quo.

REFERENCE

1. Thomas R. Shepard, Jr., "The Disaster Lobby," a talk given at the Forty-fourth Annual Meeting of the Soap and Detergent Association, New York, January 28, 1971.

4

"Coolth" Revisited

THE favored image among today's young people, and even among people who are not so young, is the individual who is "cool." This—if it has not already been replaced by something new—is the fad word, although many who apply it indiscriminately to everyone and everything from the new boy in English Lit IA to the late-model Jag in the dealer's window may be hard put to define it with any precision. Perhaps, when used to refer to a person, it might be said to mean a happy, actualized man or woman within the frame of reference of our previous chapter.

For our purposes, then, let's define "coolth" (to make it a noun) as the result of seeking out and identifying one's strengths and focusing on them—and *building* with them—in one's day-to-day living so that one is admired and respected for them.

The Fortunate and the Less Fortunate

A group that desperately seeks coolth—the "Jesus freaks"—appears so far from achieving it as to need a label and the distinguishing marks that go with it if they are to feel significant. These children of religion, many of them, seem to be embarrassed at having turned to religion—that "hang-up of the Establishment." To justify their action, their variety of religion must be different enough to get public attention. Why? Because the hard work required to gain recognition through genuine achievement takes years of disciplined study and trial and error.

What the Jesus freaks (not the Jesus people, the Jesus *freaks*) are saying as they eulogize Jesus and what He has done for them is: "Yes, You helped me—and thanks. God is great, but now I need Your name and reputation to make people know me as an individual!" They fail to remember that although Christ developed faith and a following which will outlast the ages, He sweated for it, cried for it, bled for it, and died for it. Just how many coolth seekers of this sort would die for Jesus or even give up communal live-ins for him?

Wait! Isn't it better, you may say, that religion has come into the lives of these people in some form? Certainly! But not if it merely becomes a rationale for not working and instead living in do-nothing communities in the name of "love." And this is what happens with a good number of these converts. In contrast, those who actually have found Christ and experienced spiritual stirrings feel overpowering and uncontrollable happiness; they seem to bubble over with laughter, while their senses breathe in the world and the vibrancy of earthly joys and sorrows.

The few! (But how this number is growing!) These fortunate ones do not rave, cry, and writhe on the ground. They have no need to frenetically proclaim, "Yes, I believe." They don't have to convince themselves; they radiate confidence, thus showing nonbelievers, quite calmly, their newly discovered serenity and capacity for real change and growth. (It *is* crucial in the coming years to say, "Yes, I believe"—but a valid belief must be lived as well as spoken.)

When a mind has developed little capacity for feeling, it must reach out to prove it can be exciting, original, different. What others seem to feel, consequently, the "small" man must *pretend* to feel. This he does with extra fervency, hoping he will convince others and especially himself.

Each His Own Mental Shield

Here we have a classic manifestation of the defense mechanism known as overcompensation, further illustrating the crucial need for many or all of us to increase our awareness of self—our worth, dignity, significance.

Take the cocktail party where executives and their wives flit around from group to group hoping to impress their friends and any particularly distinguished guests. Most likely the women have spent the day coping with housework, the Fuller Brush man, and school lunches; secretly, they would prefer a relaxing dinner with the family. Meanwhile, trying to impress the Country Club set, the men hide their paunches with double-breasted suits and engage in flip talk. So we have a bunch of tensed-up men and women waiting to say the right thing at the right time. The "right thing" generally consists of the latest put-down from *The New Yorker* or *Esquire,* with the farthest-out phrases filling the gaps in the lagging conversation: "Right on!" "Great!" "Aren't we having fun!" Each individual is desperately trying to assure himself that cocktail parties are *the* most and "where it's *at"!* We aren't opposed to parties at all. We're simply asking some questions about the *quality* of many of them.

Are we saying some of these people are "freaks" too? A gross exaggeration, maybe, but remember a few of the parties you've gone to? Remember how you welcomed the beginning oblivion as you picked up your first drink and turned to the man or woman at your elbow? Remember how that emotional outlet you rationalized away set you up just nicely enough to endure the boredom you knew was inevitable?

What gave you this power to foretell that boredom? A mind already sated with expedient rationales and the fear that they might be challenged. Hence the need for a mind shield.

It's a Temptation to Rationalize

To return for a moment to the younger scene, a parallel is obvious. That mind shield—the euphoric ceremonies at which frenzied initiates ejaculate "Jesus!"—provides a reason for not working to change what is continually put down. "Spend my life praising Christ? Kind of an easy life, WOW!"

So, while Mom and Pop cocktail away their guilt, the kids indulge in great orgies of jumping, squirming, and screaming. And they feel virtuous about it. "We really CARE; we're cool; we're doing what we should. Oh, yes,

we've licked our problems and turned to Jesus or to deny-
ing war or hating pollution—we have a Cause! We don't
have to think about the folks anymore, and they're happy
because their children are saved." (Please note again that
we're not talking about the *real* Jesus people, but about
the Jesus *freaks*.)

Or they sit in student unions or coffeehouses and
say, "We didn't create the world's problems—why should
we do anything to solve them?" Yet something—they don't
know just what—must be done.

Thinking about a problem, worrying about how to
cope with it, is unnecessary so long as a defense mechanism is available. It hurts to destroy this shield, but
it is deadly to keep it activated. Maybe an answer can
be found by looking for effective, mind-building mech-
anisms rather than cover-ups. Fortunately, a mind shield
will not destroy confidence as quickly as dwelling upon
negatives because the corroded positives are replaced by
a void, rather than an evil.

The solution? Stop and listen before you speak. If what
you are about to say sounds like rationalization, wait, search
your mind for a strength, and relate to that. Instead of
eroding what confidence you may have by covering up or
vocalizing weaknesses, begin to rebuild strong ideas and
motives. Bring them to the surface and expand them to
fill the void that will be left when you no longer say, "I'm
not, and I can't help it." Find the strength to say, "I *am*,
I *did*, I'll *do*," and others will begin to think, "He *is*, he
does, he'll *take responsibility*." It works both ways—from
parent to child and from child to parent; from manager
to subordinate and from subordinate to manager. Precedent
says the junior must learn from the senior. *Can* such a
belief ever be replaced by reciprocal agreement to be

guided by the friendship and trust implicit in true listening?

Those Opinion Polls

The tendency to overreact to the latest poll or source of comment and leap to simplistic conclusions is always with us. For instance:

"Business is no damned good."

"Big organizations are strangling the country."

"All that is great and American has stemmed from economic free enterprise."

"The businessman is the giant of our time."

"This is the greatest generation of young people in history."

"Kids today are just no damned good."

"Only 3 to 4 percent of young people are radicals."

"Survey shows 78 percent of young people in their teens are radicals."

"Young people in business are afraid of a challenge."

"Young people in business are chafing for great challenge."

What we need here is rational assessment—listening before we speak and, above all, listening to *hear*. We're saying, then, that quick, simplistic reactions are expedient. We're also saying that perpetual listening, with no response, is expedient. A wise blend of patience, tolerance, careful evaluation, and finally the courage to state one's views affirmatively and link them to objectives, timetables, and *action* provides the key to distinguishing between expedience and expertise.

Arnold Toynbee's monumental *A Study of History,* which reviews the rise and fall of civilizations thus far known to man, reaches some conclusions which should not surprise us. His research, for example, indicates that civilizations develop "in response to a challenge of special difficulty which rouses man to make an unprecedented effort." He says further that a successful response to such a challenge is more likely to occur in a "hard" rather than an "easy" environment.

We submit "tough" as a substitute for "hard" in this context. Whichever term you prefer, Toynbee bears out the contention of this book that no success in the real sense of the word is probable without obstacles to be overcome along the way—a truism which should be all too familiar (but often seems elusive, because it's *tough*) to any top executive.

A Pattern for Change

As individuals and citizens, let us

1. Actively seek the involvement of businessmen and other organizational leaders and thought shapers and their commitment to massively accelerated patterns of exchange.
2. In fulfillment of this, insure—at the very least—more summer employment of faculty by business and other organizations and a significant increase in visits to elementary schools, secondary schools, and universities (for lectures, symposia, workshops, and the like) by business, government, social, and religious leaders.

3. Insist that business managers in particular carefully escalate what is now a promising start in the direction of this essential exchange.
4. Target imaginative research to determine the validity of the thesis that all people have the duty (to themselves and to society) to attempt something beyond their apparent level of competence—that they should be guaranteed the right to fail. The corollary here, of course, is that they must be given the opportunity to discover new mental, physical, and spiritual muscle—true human significance, true self-actualization.

As a start, make a list of several difficult things you are going to face up to during the next year and break the confrontational steps down into "bite-size" segments. Then *begin.*

5

High Expectations

There is yet another factor in the parent/child, employer/employee relationship which is crucial to the quality of that relationship and the satisfactions to be derived from it. This is the matter of expectations.

The balance here is precarious. Both sides ought to profit, yet both appear to forget at times that the benefits should flow in two directions. In an age of affluence, the well-known desire of American parents to give their children more advantages than they themselves ever had may have gotten a little out of hand; the children frequently seem to receive but not give—and complain that the parents don't really understand them or provide the no-questions-asked support they are entitled to. In the same way, employers who offer top wages and, they believe, ideal working conditions may find that they get little in return—and the employees growl belligerently about exploitation.

That Missing Element

What they overlook is that without expectations the results are bound to be disappointing. No matter how generous Father may be with the family car, Jack will probably not be a careful driver if Father gives no signs of expecting him to drive carefully and in fact expects the worst—particularly if Jack doesn't feel deep down inside that he at least partially earned the right to use the car. No matter what a luxuriant growth of "fringes" a company makes available, employees will seldom exert themselves if the supervisor automatically assumes they are no-good loafers. (Again it works both ways: Parents whose children appear to expect nothing of them, and organizations whose employees seem equally indifferent, will soon start projecting the looked-for image.) Within reason—because expectations must of course be realistic—the higher the expectations, the greater the results. And, unfortunately, vice versa. One of the greatest fallacies at the root of many abortive "employee benefits programs" is the idea that people want something for nothing. They *don't!*

Take a searching look at the typical organization in the United States, whether business, governmental, educational, religious, or military. You will find in at least 80 percent of the cases a widely prevalent mystique, misunderstanding, pliant palliative, protean placebo, call it what you will. This is the belief that we show regard, concern, friendship, brotherhood, and/or that tired phrase "good employee relations" when we proffer the benefit basket and reward employees for considerably less than their top efforts. Thus, in reality we destroy the stuff of dignity and self-respect.

The manager of an organizational unit—or a parent

or a teacher—communicates much more than he *says*. High performance expectations are a splendid way to show his confidence in others, but the confidence of his employees, children, or pupils in his integrity is a precious gift he must first acquire. When he declares, "You expect more from XYZ (or from us, your family, or this course you are taking) and you'll get it," he must be able to prove it by his own attitude and record.

The Search for Excellence

"I was told I must produce *excellence*. That's why I'm here in America now," said a 22-year-old Austrian. His father had been killed flying a plane two years before, and this young man needed to go to school. With no money, he had to *deserve* his education. When he applied for admission to the aviation/military school, he was told that it would cost him a small fortune unless he could produce the same excellence his father had shown. He must attain top-notch ratings in both studies and sporting events. He did—because the headmaster demanded his very best. He became top aviator at the school; and eventually, because of his scholastic excellence, he was sent to the United States as the school's representative. In the process he learned to respect himself, which is necessary fuel for the continuous pursuit of excellence.

Aristotle said, "Lose yourself in productive work—in a way of excellence." And a search of the Scriptures reveals such parallel truths as this statement of Jesus: "Ask, and it shall be given you. Seek, and ye shall find; knock, and it shall be opened unto you." These great men expected much from themselves and from other people—in that order. The young Austrian is only one of many (but not enough) individuals currently committed to excellence.

So many young people unthinkingly reject the search for excellence and accept as revealed truth the put-downs of a Jerry Rubin: "The university is a place for making it—a high-pressured rat race. Competition for grades, degrees, recommendations, getting into graduate school, and getting a good job. The academic world is a hierarchy, and everybody's always kissing the ass of the guy on top of him." [1] In fact, ". . . the goal is to castrate students." [2] Students feel these words are vibrant and exciting—A NEW WAY!

Yes, a virile society can be castrated when its taproot— Judeo-Christianity—is assaulted with sickening insistence by second-rate secularism as in the much-acclaimed *Jesus Christ, Superstar*. But let's abruptly change terminology, tempo, and target and quote from a poem*—in the same young, modern idiom—that was deliberately written in response to the challenge thrown down by the original lyrics.

> Oh, Jesus Christ, you crazy man . . .
> What made You rise to live again?
> Can You still love these lives we lead
> Of pain and hate and greed?
> Or is there something we don't know,
> A fire that sets Your soul aglow?
>
> Oh, come on, Jesus . . . You aren't king.
> Where's that immortal life You bring? . . .

---

* This poem is the work of Gail Batten. It is reproduced in full in Appendix A.

And the reply:

> O.K., you call me Superstar. . . .
> I don't get drunk or go too far.
> But do I ever put you down
> For taking time to mess around?
> I don't condone the narrow life
> All filled with toil and fear and strife.
> My task on earth's no simple one,
> To show you God can be great fun.
>
> I know you laugh—you play it cool
> And think me one gigantic fool.
> But do you really understand
> What it's like at God's right hand?
> Come on, you say, "Why should we pray?
> Walk piously around all day?"
> I fear you all don't really see
> That gift God gave to you and me . . .

A tough Jesus, in other words, is believable to some only as one of the world's greater philosophers, as the historical Jesus, not as the Christ whose dreams, zest for life, and determination to dwell on strengths are implicit in the message which He challenged the Disciples to spread and which has survived the fall of nations, the reign of terrorists and anarchists, and the repeated upsurge of evil ideas throughout history.

Along with this message have endured the teachings of men like Aristotle, Plato, Socrates, Jefferson, Emerson, and now a newer wave: Gandhi, Martin Luther King, Gibran. All these men have based their philosophy on knowledge of one's capabilities through confrontation, on respect for self and love of others, and on the importance of building a solid foundation of values to live by—in short, the pursuit of excellence—demonstrating in the process why they were happy men in the real sense of the word. Action replaced verbiage, and attitudes assumed a positive direction.

My Brother's Keeper

"Am I my brother's keeper?" Cain asked the Lord after killing his brother Abel. As indeed we are in the sense intended in Genesis. But we try too hard to play the role which we read into this often-quoted question. Rather, we ought to play the much tougher role of "brother's brother" and *help him to keep himself*—in other words, be true to the way of excellence.

The president of a food-products company was facing emotional and physical collapse. His staff, too, were in poor health. One had a heart condition, one was receiving psychiatric therapy, another had suffered a mild paralytic stroke—and everybody was feeling extreme tension. The chief executive was convinced that the tension was being caused by two locals of a large international union. However, he was puzzled. "I really can't understand it," he mused. "Every year we go into negotiations with the most carefully compiled industry and area data to prove why we can't give any more—and still we are forced to concede a little more each year. We've painted ourselves into a corner. We don't have many management prerogatives left. When negotiations are over, the agreement is usually several months retroactive, and then it's time to prepare for negotiations again. We simply can't go on like this."

Why this state of affairs? Simply stated, it had never occurred to top management in this company that it would be good human relations to express through its policies and procedures and practices a belief that employees were being paid to do their very best. Words like "high expectations" were alien to these men's ears. They did not encourage excellence. They honestly believed that sound human relations called for pandering, in effect, to the supposed needs of their employees—for being "nice." They had learned from human relations books and seminars that every employee craved security, recognition, opportunity, and belonging and that a reasonable benefit package would keep him loyal, happy, and grateful. They were literally trying to be their brother's—or at least their employee's—keeper.

But benefits cost money—more each year. So, every time, management would go into negotiations prepared to point out why the flow must be slowed down for the sake of the company P&L statement. Naturally it soon found itself in a situation very like that of the overly indulgent parent who is trying to withdraw luxuries to which his child has become accustomed. There was the typical petulant response, followed by the inevitable bafflement, frustration, anger, and finger pointing.

Management was counseled to take the existing one-year contracts—which reflected a sad and dismal story of constant concessions over a period of years—and put them in a lower drawer, out of sight. Completely new contracts were then drafted, the company indicating in each instance that it would expect the agreement to remain in force for three years and also requesting that the union make a substantial number of concessions. In one case, the company requested 18 concessions and, to its great surprise, obtained 12, including the three-year contract. From the other local, management received 14 concessions out of 23, again including the longer contract term.

Concern Only for Full Effort

As all the various "P"s in the organization were re-viewed—philosophy, policies, procedures, practices, prin-ciples, processes, privileges—the company's bulletin boards, staff meetings, house organ, and other methods of in-house communication were thoroughly overhauled so that the employees began to receive a message of high expectations, of emphasis on excellence. They were told in every way possible that the company's concern for their individual dignity and worth would be reflected in new procedures designed to compensate them only for results, only for *the demonstrated use of their full abilities*. This change from a permissive climate to one of high expectations was in no sense accomplished overnight. The first months brought no great degree of mutual satisfaction; by the end of approximately three years, however, there had been a discernible increase in the beat and tempo of activity, in individual pride of achievement, and in the prevailing respect for dignity and worth of both employees and management.

The dolorous history of this company also included the fact that a number of young M.B.A.s recruited into the management development program had departed after just a few months or, at best, two or three years. A search-ing examination revealed that a principal reason for this was that each young recruit felt that he was being *cared for* rather than *challenged*. That he was being given some-thing he had not earned. That he was not going to have to reach into his inner resources and find new strengths and new talents and a new ability to cope. The management development program was accordingly revised so that it reflected, both in its in-house operations and in its campus-recruiting aspects, a much more spare and lean approach. A tough and even demanding set of standards, the potential executive was informed, would be "applied with great consistency once he became a member of the company." The most crucial change, however, was that management began to stress (and practice) this need for positive, enlightened management by example and to set an example of excellence.

Interestingly, many of the young men who had previously applied for positions with this company had represented a type which no longer showed up in the university placement offices for interview. They were prescreened by the tough-minded and demanding criteria listed as preconditions for employment. They preferred not to stretch, not to grow by continually confronting unfamiliar situations and difficulties. The young people who replaced them were as tough as the exacting standards they welcomed; they were eager to discover new strengths, new abilities within themselves. Make no mistake about it, there are many of these tough-minded young people. But few can demonstrate these attributes in the absence of sufficiently high expectations.

The Future Is *Now*

In a synthesis of the research and findings of the late Dr. Abraham Maslow, *The Third Force,* Frank Goble gives an account of something that happened to this much quoted psychologist shortly before his death:

> In a recent interview Dr. Maslow spoke of the so-called generation gap, expressing sadness that youngsters, radical youngsters and hippies, in particular, are searching so hard for truth, honesty, beauty and brotherhood. "And I would say to them, for the love of Pete it is already existing. You are searching for some kind of future and it is here and it is now. All you have to do is turn to it." [3]

It's less trouble to talk and live as though one's external environment were at fault. In contrast, looking inward for God-given potential and outward and upward for goals to actualize this potential *can* be tough—but good.

Coping with Today's Unease

The young person in business appears today to be in a somewhat uneasy mood. The perceptive and widely quoted Daniel Yankelovich described him in an address to the Institute of Life Insurance at their annual meeting:

> . . . After two years of work he has become a little critical of the company (although he keeps his criticism to himself). He's a little less sure of himself; he's not moving as fast as he thought he would be. He hasn't been able to effect as many things as he thought he would. He is bothered by make-work, by the jockeying for position. He feels pretty remote from where the action is. Not enough is demanded of him to let him *test himself*. [Italics ours.] He is giving less than he has to give.

And elsewhere in the same speech:

> It is this combination of the diminished motivation in the individual and greater complexity in the organization that creates the problem I am trying to define. In visualizing it

we must discard stereotypes. This young fellow is not a callow organization man—faceless, unabrasive, finding safety only in the anonymity of the machine. He's not a timid Caspar Milquetoast, withdrawing from the rigors of a man's world to the maternal retreat of the home. He's not the alienated man, living out a lie and secretly condemning the society and its values. He is a surprisingly mature, well-trained, well-educated, secure, realistic fellow with lots of energy, with an *intense need to be tested* and to succeed at something, and with a readiness to dedicate himself to something bigger than himself. [Italics ours.] Yet, somehow it is not possible for him to do so.[4]

Dr. Yankelovich has made some tough-minded and telling points here—points which ought to challenge industry and other organizational leaders thoroughly. Indeed, the extent to which top management understands and copes with this uneasy state of mind—overt or unspoken—within its younger recruits may well determine its very survival in the next few years.

In Deed as Well as Word

What can we do about it? Well, for one thing, more organizations ought to become expectations- and goal-oriented in deed as well as word. Goals ought to be set throughout the entire organization—at every functional level and in every individual job where it is at all possible. It should also be well understood that the formulation, dissemination, and communication of a carefully worked out philosophy are an important prelude to goal setting because this supplies the conceptual framework, the timeless values and principles which the more specific goals and objectives are designed to accomplish.

Evidence continues to surface—if you look for it—that today's young manager is no different *fundamentally* from his precedessors. True, he's more vocal, freer, and in some cases better equipped, but he still needs goals and he will still respond to them. Here are some telling excerpts from Judson Gooding's article in *Fortune* entitled "The Accelerated Generation Moves into Management":

> Today's junior managers . . . reflect the passionate concerns of youth in the 1970s—for individuality, openness, humanism, concern and change—and they are determined to be heard.

> Some corporations are actively encouraging them to make the fullest contributions possible [high expectations] and are benefiting handsomely from the fizz of new ideas they generate.[5]

In brief, these young men are being challenged by high expectations—and liking "the freedom to make mistakes, an opportunity for responsibility without having to grab to get it." They say, according to Mr. Gooding, "If you stifle people in my age group you're going to lose them." And, "You have to be given the opportunity to fail in order to grow."

What we need, as should be obvious on every page of this book, is high, stretching goals and standards for both the young and the not so young and the confidence—in self and others—that will make possible their achievement. To which must be added the assurance that managers at all levels will be better trained in individual strength actualization and the habit of dedicated commitment in word and deed alike. We must stimulate, by every means we can, better preparation for the "whole person" development that is so sorely lacking in a society which seems to be increasingly beset by cleavage and fragmentation. Such cleavage is utterly unnecessary!

A Pattern for Change

We desperately need

1. Research into what happens to the soul of an individual when he is "kept" or is "given" what he has the capacity—however dormant—to earn.
2. Job enrichment (or what is usually understood by that term). This is only a start, however. We are calling here for large sums of money to support research that will suggest better ways of helping to develop the *total personality* and will give us new insight into individual strength, dignity, and potential. In short, "total individual" enrichment.
3. Imaginatively programmed applications of these findings to the purposes, principles, policies, procedures, processes, and practices of all our organizations.

To make a modest start on your own initiative, why not visit one educator, one clergyman, one politician, and any other such "thought shapers" in your local community and try to find out what they really think about man's nature? Don't they assume people are fundamentally good? Do they think (*a la* B. F. Skinner) that man is simply a rather advanced animal—or do they assume that every individual is the unique, splendid creation of a living God? Think about the implications of the answers you get in terms of our plea for greater knowledge of the human soul.

REFERENCES

1. Jerry Rubin, *Do It* (New York: Simon & Schuster, 1970), p. 25.
2. Ibid., p. 28.
3. Frank Goble, *The Third Force: The Psychology of Abraham Maslow,* Copyright 1970 by Thomas Jefferson Research Center, all rights reserved. Reprinted by permission of Grossman Publishers, Inc.
4. Daniel Yankelovich, "Today's Young Adults: A Growing Business Problem," *Personnel* (March–April 1966).
5. Judson Gooding, "The Accelerated Generation Moves into Management," *Fortune* (March 1971). Used by permission.

6

Compassion and Beyond

IN this book we have been preaching concern for individual dignity, worth, and potential. However, our concern may not "go down" very well with the individuals involved —that is, it may not be acceptable—unless it is accompanied by *compassion*.

What do we mean by compassion? Literally a "suffering with"; as Webster puts it, "a sympathetic consciousness of others' distress together with a desire to alleviate it." "Distress" is perhaps a pretty strong word in our context, but we *are* talking about a sensitivity to other people's feelings and problems. There is nothing effeminate about it; it is both a manly and a womanly emotion.

When compassion is not real, when it is mere pity or condescension, it is exceedingly hard for the object of the compassion not to resent it. Also, even when it is genuine, it is exceedingly hard for the compassionate person to communicate it and—most of all—to live with it. For it leaves the mind vulnerable to growth, to remaining and expanding on the path of sensitivity. To be sensitive is to know that the cool way is not the easy way, so that the pursuit of individual or corporate coolth is seen as an expediently stitched-together fabric of compromise.

For a Better World

Perhaps what is called for is a revolution of sorts. It may be, in fact, that this really is a book on revolution— *a revolution based on compassion.*

This should not be so shocking. We hear a great deal these days about how, ostensibly, a revolution is now being propagated by many young and not-so-young radicals to overturn our society. "We must become more open," they say. "We must care more. We must have liberty to do our own thing." At least they allege that this is the essence of their philosophy, but let's see what Jerry Rubin tells the world in *Do It:*

> We Yippies are cocky because we know history will absolve us. The history books will see us—the freaks, not the straights —as the heroes of the 1970s. We know that because we are going to write the history books. The goal is to turn on everybody who can be turned on, and turn off everybody else. Theatre has no rules, forms, structures, standards, traditions—it is pure, natural energy impulse anarchy. The job of the revolution is to smash stage sets, start fires in movie theatres and then scream "fire." The theatrical geniuses of today are creating the drum of Viet Nam in occupied school administration buildings across America. The Living Theatre a far-out guerilla group came to Berkeley while people were fighting the National Guard in the streets. As Pacifists, they opposed the street action. Living Theatre eliminated the stage and joined the audience

revolutionary theatre. "I am not allowed to smoke marijuana," one Living Theatre member sobbed. He was offered
five joints. Another cry: "I can't take off my clothes." Around
him people stripped naked. At the end of the performance
everyone left to take the revolution to the streets. The cast
stopped at the front door. . . .[1]

And, speaking of another episode,

The boy editors just did not understand just how conspira-
torial we Yippies are. We infiltrated their program committee to set up a rigged debate for the afternoon: "Should
college newspaper editors association take a stand on the
war?" That morning we all dropped acid and got ready for
battle.[2]

Considerable confusion here, and overtones of violence,
but little real compassion and certainly no readiness to
compromise.

For a second modern approach to what might be loosely
termed "revolution," let's quote again from *The Third
Force*. Here is how author Goble explains the Maslow
concept of the good society:

For such a society to work it is necessary for the citizens
to have the ability to choose efficient leaders. The ability
to detect actual superiority. This need to be coupled with
a minimum of jealousy and antagonism toward the superior
leaders. The synergic society or what Maslow in his later
works referred to as the Eupsychian society is a society which
creates an environment where people can develop their
potential and satisfy their innate psychological needs. The
good society is one which is fulfilling and makes self-
actualization possible. "A healthy society would be one
which fulfills the most potentialities of the greatest number
of men."

Maslow flatly rejects the idea that the interest of the individual and his society are necessarily mutually exclusive
and antagonistic. This is a basic premise of Freudian theory.

Maslow envisions a society with psychologically healthy people, where there will be less crime, less mental illness, less need for restrictive legislation. Such a society, rather than protecting itself from people's instincts as Freud saw it, would encourage the strengthening of instincts and would encourage people to develop their potential for love, cooperation, achievement and growth.[3]

A more sober and reasoned analysis, certainly. What is perhaps a matter for concern here is the fact that one suspects man is to create his ideal society by secular means alone; in other words, revolution—or evolution—is to be achieved through the new psychology and our advancing technology.

For a third approach, however, let's turn to *Revolution Now,* a book by Bill Bright:

Science cannot perform miracles. Technicians may attempt to and they actually do accomplish the incredible but they cannot accomplish the impossible. Only God can. And God's greatest miracle is the transformation of a life. Intellectually brilliant, ruthlessly ambitious, fanatically religious—this was Saul of Tarsus. Utterly devoted to the annihilation of the Christian faith, he became a bloody robot of destruction. Compassion, pity, mercy, these had long since died in the soul of this Jewish zealot. Sex and age meant nothing to him, he existed only to kill and destroy. And then he saw a Light, and he heard a Voice. For the first time there burst from his lips an expression of submission, "Lord." The master was mastered. The prosecutor was arrested. The steel was melted and the stone shattered. The proud, ruthless prosecutor became the willing bondslave of the One he had attacked. The life of violence and murder became a life of compassion and love.[4]

In short, it is compassion alone—with no trace of expediency or compromise—that can truly achieve a better world.

Back to the Old Values

Admittedly, our attempts to extract the core of Messrs. Rubin's, Maslow's, and Bright's thinking may not have arrived at what these gentlemen themselves would characterize as the quintessential basis of their respective approaches. Granted that there is this difficulty, let's nevertheless see what we can develop through a process of analysis, evaluation, synthesis, and synergy.

Analysis, evaluation, synthesis, and synergy. These words sound so sophisticated, so complicated and even esoteric. But need they be?

ANALYSIS: *Breaking a thing into its component parts.*

- What is promised by each approach?
- What is threatened by each approach?

EVALUATION: *Attaching value to the components of something previously analyzed.*

- What is beautiful in each?
- What is ugly in each?
- What is each for?
- What is each against?
- What elements in each contribute to *building?*
- What elements in each contribute to *destruction?*

SYNTHESIS: *Combining often diverse concepts into a coherent whole.*

- Which approach involves the most *giving?*
- Which approach involves the most *taking?*
- Which contains those elements most conducive to growth?

- Which contains those elements most conducive to retardation?
- Which promises the most consonance?
- Which best lends itself to dissatisfaction?
- Which best lends itself to satisfaction?

SYNERGY: *Combining action or operation so that the whole is greater than the sum of the parts.*

- Which is most explosive?
- Which is most implosive?
- Which would seem to possess the greatest capacity for acting in concert?
- Which best illustrates values which are mutually supportive and reinforcing?

And so on. Is there any need to spell it out? Rubin's concept appears sick, Maslow's incomplete. Our true goal must be revolution in the best and most wholesome sense of the word, revolution motivated by compassion; and such a revolution can be effectively planned, organized, actuated, coordinated, and controlled. And the all-important starting place is values and beliefs, with compassion paramount.

Setting the Other Person Free

Implicit in compassion is *love*. This is obvious in the story of a young girl of 14, whose parents were wealthy and busy. One day she said wistfully about a friend, also 14, "Her parents sure must love her." The girl she meant was being carried off the snowy slopes of a ski run. She had fallen on the trail and somehow twisted, perhaps fractured, her left ankle. Since she'd had other, less serious falls, the remark could have been intended sarcastically, but it was not. The girl who had spoken had parents who sheltered and protected her until she felt like a frustrated china doll. She had been very active as a little girl, participating in gymnastics and many sports, but while practicing in the gym one afternoon she had flipped onto the cement floor and injured her spine. Now that she was able to stand and walk normally, her parents showered her with clothes and money to buy fun, but forbade her to participate in any activity in which she might possibly injure herself once more.

Superficially, it sounds ludicrous for this girl to feel that her friend's parents loved their daughter more, but stop and think. The other girl's parents allowed her the freedom to choose the activities which gave her the most self-actualization. Though they admitted that they agonized privately over their child's repeated falls, they let her go on skiing. They contented themselves with tempering her enthusiasm with a few sensible restraints—in the full wisdom of people who know that an individual can't be really happy unless he does what he dreams of doing. They understood the principle that to be really good you must be able to get up after each discouragement; that, with each problem conquered, a stronger and more resilient spirit will gain strength.

The parents of the "china doll" put their own fear first and thought of the pain *they* would feel if the girl was hurt again. They didn't think that perhaps her dream of being an accomplished sportswoman was being thwarted; perhaps they didn't think it mattered very much. Who was showing real love? All four individuals loved their daughters, but the parents who loved selfishly were hindering a girl's growth in confidence and ability by placing their own needs before the fulfillment of someone who had yet to discover that she really could cope with challenge.

The love that is the heart and soul of compassion is unselfish. It sets the other person free to learn and develop as an individual, even if he hurts himself in doing so, and to use his talents to change what needs changing in the world around him. To promote revolution if he must.

What Are You Doing to Help?

Arnold Toynbee lists five characteristics of the last five minutes of a declining civilization: atheism, materialism, alcoholism, homosexuality, and socialism. All these he feels are demonstrably detrimental to a viable enduring society. All are much too familiar today. As an aspiring, evolving, or even (hopefully) mature person, what are *you* doing about combating them?

The direction of our society as a whole is determined by the aggregate of its existing organizations—of whatever type. These organizations are aggregates of individuals, and individuals are aggregates of individual talents. So what kind of example are you setting? What is it saying to the world?

You manager! What is your department or division doing to develop and put to use principles, policies, procedures, processes, and practices that will counteract the degenerative forces of which the phenomena cited by Toynbee are the outward symptoms?

"We must have change!" "The Establishment must crumble!" "We reject your values!" "Down with the System!" Such are the cries not only of many campus militants but also of some young managerial people. (In corporations, of course, these sentiments are expressed in a hedged, cautious, and frequently cynical manner.)

Are the shouts and slogans justified? Are they sincere? *Are they informed?* Do they reflect the true state of the world? Before society attempts to answer these questions, two others—highly important at this juncture—need to be explored thoroughly:

1. Have the great truths of the Ten Commandments, the Sermon on the Mount, and the U.S. Constitution been tried and found wanting in relevance, integrity, and worth? (These are the fundamental source of the pattern of life in our *American* society. We are not relegating to limbo the scriptural and legal manifestos of other nations.) In short, have we truly tested the validity of the truths that are our heritage as a people? Or

2. Have we, as fallible human beings, simply failed to develop a sufficient supply of methods, systems, or just plain *ideas?* (We define a new idea as "the relevant, updated application of a timeless truth.")

We know of no new truths which have been "discovered" or "created" in the past 1,900 years. New ideas? Yes! New methods? Yes! New understanding? Yes! But truths? No! The works of Adam Smith, John Calvin, and others have been significant indeed, but they consisted only in new applications of the truths that already *were*.

So the central thrust of our challenge is to consider the patent futility of simply "putting down" values which may not have yielded their optimum payload as yet. Rather, we must concentrate our enormous energies—and they *are* enormous—on the quest for new methods, new ideas, new understanding. This challenge takes guts. Leave it alone, then, if you are simply a shrill, cynical complainer.

A Pattern for Change

Let's think about

1. Government appointment of a "Committee for Planned Revolution" to accomplish:
   a. The clear definition and communication of national goals (in the international as well as the domestic area), so that all citizens may know what we as a nation are *for*.
   b. A comprehensive assessment and compilation of the basic values, attitudes, and beliefs which have undergirded the growth and success of the United States. This includes the cornerstone of our system of jurisprudence, which says that all men are innocent until proved guilty. It should *not* be interpreted as a placid review of "great and noble verities." Such an assessment, on the contrary, should lead to increased dissatisfaction with the status quo and a restless urge to better understand, teach, and apply tested values.
2. New and ingenious educational software (the hardware is now getting better at a fantastic rate). This should include methods of freeing new potential and imaginative ways of producing the mind toughening that grows out of confronting difficulties. It may perhaps be redundant to add that such mind toughening may well be a *right* which is being denied to vast numbers of people caught up in the often sad syndrome of "niceness." And niceness can be such a convenient expedient for avoiding real growth and change.
3. A new government department whose mission is to

stimulate the quest for greater knowledge of human potential and its utilization. A vastly better understanding of the fully functioning individual is essential to the steady building of a fully functioning society.

For yourself:

- Write your Congressman.
- Organize your own "task force" to grow new taproots at the local level for a more truly compassionate yet tough-minded society.
- If you dare, personally visit a prison or jail. Scrupulously avoid reacting to the symptoms of our present system of "reform" which you see on the premises and in the prisons. Instead, ask yourself: "What *caused* this?"

REFERENCES

1. Jerry Rubin, *Do It* (New York: Simon & Schuster, 1970), p. 130. Copyright © 1970 by the Social Education Foundation.
2. Ibid., pp. 132–133.
3. Frank Goble, op. cit.
4. William Bright, *Revolution Now*. Printed by permission, Copyright © Campus Crusade for Christ, Inc., 1969, all rights reserved.

7

Can You Hear Me?

It goes without saying that to achieve the magnificent kind of revolution in human relations we have been talking about, we are going to have to improve the effectiveness with which we communicate with one another. This goes for communication between parent and child, supervisor and supervised, management (so called) and labor. Despite the fact that the stream of books published in the communications area over the past 25 years shows no signs of drying up, we seem to be learning little from them. "Are you listening?" we ask the other fellow repeatedly. "Can you hear me?" Yet the confidence chasm—needlessly—appears wider than ever before.

Why?

Stereotypes and Dialogues

One of the most consistent, pervasive, and insidious obstacles to real communication is the tendency (and we are all guilty of this, regardless of age or position) to devise a label, a handle, a nickname for an individual or a group. Thus: "hippie," "square," "Mom," "the Old Man," "Communist," "young punks," "the Establishment," "the Union." Then we insist on speaking to that stereotype without really bothering to hear what the individual or the group may be telling us. It's easier, you see. A categorized "thing" can never threaten us, but a living, changing, unpredictable skinful of variables—that is, a person—can seem to be a menace.

Too many of us spend too much time in dialogue with our stereotypes. (Once more we define "dialogue" as "two or more people engaged in monologues," and "communication" as "shared memory, shared understanding.") Each party is afraid to hear what the other is trying to say. When the guard has been dropped, and the stereotype is seen for a real human being, true communication can take place. Then, and only then, can negatives as well as positives be faced. The idea here is to listen to one another; to perceive existing weaknesses in a context of discovery, discussion, and use of present and yet-to-be developed strengths.

You *Say* You're Listening . . .

A personnel director in a large Midwestern organization had just returned from a Chicago seminar concerned with how to develop better communications. His 21-year-old son was visiting with him. After about 15 minutes the boy stopped and said, "Dad, you're *really listening* to me!" And, as the father put it, "I really *was* listening to him more than I ever had. While in Chicago I apparently learned the knack."

The personnel director seemed to marvel at this—even though, in his job, "real" listening would seem to be a top-priority skill. "Here I am in my fifties," he explained, "and for some reason I've just now learned how to really listen. And, more important, how to really *hear*. And you know what? I think, from here on, life in all its dimensions is going to be a lot more fun."

Take a second case—that of a high school senior who faithfully participated in church activities. One day she suddenly called her Sunday School teacher and asked to meet him downtown; there was something, she said, that she wanted to discuss. The teacher, who was a businessman, left his office and met the girl. She confessed an indiscretion—intimacy with her boyfriend—and added that she felt too guilty to continue coming to church.

Instead of "pious" reproof and criticism, this young girl received understanding. After hearing her tearful vow not to repeat this experiment in premarital sex, the teacher assured her that he respected and admired her all the more for that decision. She returned to Sunday School with her boyfriend and attended church services regularly; the indiscretion was never again mentioned. The couple are now married, have two children, and seem to be enjoying a fine, happy existence.

It's Hard to Say "I'm Sorry"

The board chairman of a large, wealthy, long-established organization was concerned because his son—now in his early thirties—was functioning only adequately as head of a relatively modest division within the total structure of the company. The father expressed great disappointment. "I made sure," he said, "that Jim had the finest formal education possible: an engineering degree from M.I.T. and an M.B.A. from the Harvard Graduate School of Business. Somehow, though, Jim doesn't quite live up to what I had fondly hoped was his potential. I've got to confess I'm baffled."

In a subsequent conversation, the son revealed a great deal of frustration—a feeling verging on bitterness. "My dad doesn't really have any idea what my abilities are," Jim declared. "He's always looked at me and seen faults, criticized my weaknesses. I used to be pretty sure that he thought a lot of me and was simply being critical so as to prepare me for taking on a good job. But I really think he's started believing that I have a lot more weaknesses than I have strengths. I don't really know how I can get to him. If I try to tell him anything about myself, he immediately says that one of my weaknesses is arrogance and conceit."

The young man had tears in his eyes. "I simply don't know how to cope with the situation," he owned. "Dad has a stereotype of me—a fixed image—that nothing seems to be able to change."

A counselor arranged for the two to meet at a downtown club where they were members. In a private room where there was no possibility of interruption, a climate of candor was established in which the board chairman and his son were encouraged to drop their guard, to air repressed feelings about each other. As the conversation began to unfold, both men became somewhat emotional. Both confessed that they loved each other deeply but, for some reason, had felt constrained to communicate within a stereotyped context of criticism.

To establish true communication between these two, several meetings were in fact necessary. After hours of talk, Jim and his father were able to look at each other and converse frankly and openly. They began to realize that commenting with unsuppressed admiration and candor on one another's strengths was in no way effeminate or unbusinesslike but, in reality, took more courage than pointing out one another's weaknesses. In fact, they discovered that this kind of open-minded listening—plus the courage to say "I'm sorry" when necessary—was probably the only real and lasting way to cope properly with those supposed faults which had plagued each about the other.

Condemnation—Wholesale

At a cocktail party, some 20 people were gathered, most of them in their early, middle, or late forties. A few were in their early fifties. The conversation soon swung, predictably, to a discussion of "our young people." Soon it seemed to be totally devoted to pointing out the faults, the inadequacies, the reprehensible conduct and attitudes of *all* the young people in the country today—especially their immature tendency (regardless of chronological age) to rely on overly simplified and sweepingly general bromides of despair.

At this point, one man spoke up. "Look, I'm getting tired of this whole thing," he said. "I, for one, believe that we have a great many very fine young people, and I don't really give a damn about how long their hair may be." "That is," he added hurriedly, "I refuse to *judge* them by the length of their hair. Actually, I'm like all the rest of you. I don't like to see a boy looking like a girl."

By this time, both emotions and the quantity of liquor consumed had created a highly subjective and volatile atmosphere. Another man snapped, "Why don't you quit talking out of both sides of your mouth at once?" And, seconded by his wife, he went on to make the point that the man seemed to have an ambivalent, indecisive outlook on today's youth.

The first man shrugged, then simply repeated his statement: "I do not *like* long hair on a boy, but I will not condemn him on the basis of anything so superficial."

Here I believe we can perceive a pattern, a conversational syndrome all too typical of our times. What was really happening in this room? These men and women were indeed condemning young people on the basis of a single—to them abhorrent—characteristic. In this case, hair. Moreover, by their wholesale condemnation they were widening the chasm between the generations.

Are You Part of the Problem?

So often our negative, corrosive comments about the problems of our society or a "people" problem on the job can quickly make us *part* of that problem. And this works both ways. The young person "into" drugs for the nobly stated purpose of "understanding the problem" is no different from the manager who seeks to "understand" alcoholism by drinking six martinis every day. Or vice versa.

The following statement comes from *Youth and the Establishment,* a report on research for John D. Rocke-

feller 3rd and the Task Force on Youth by Daniel Yankelovich Inc. The speaker is a young Californian now attend-
ing a university in Missouri; she is describing how she
has changed almost against her will in response to criticism from her elders. "I have changed a lot in the past few
years. Essentially I am still sort of a 'square' liberal—but
I do feel my ideals are probably a lot different than they
used to be. I feel a much stronger allegiance to my generation than I did before. It's the adults, even more than
Nixon and the war, who have forced me to take sides." [1]

What's really happening here? To answer this question,
let's make some statements of our own and see what we
come up with.

1. Among the various lower creatures, those who have
    some of the strongest tendencies to cluster together
    are domestic sheep and geese. *Why?*
2. The executive who seemingly can relax or feel se-
    cure only in a business meeting or at a party, or
    surrounded by aides or friends of his own persuasion,
    is lacking in some substantial stuff of the mind or
    spirit. *What?*
3. The student who can turn on, relax, or feel secure
    only with his peers in a "rap" session or similar form
    of despair-centered intellectual incest is lacking some
    substantial stuff of the mind or spirit. *What?*
4. Does the real individual (the compleat self-actualizer)
    require such external stimuli? Or does he possess
    internal stuff and fiber? *Why? Why not?*

The kind of communication that will remedy the problems
implicit in these four statements is of course complex; it
cannot be viewed simplistically. A beginning will have been

77

made, however, when we understand that the real purpose of criticism is to search for hidden yet potential strengths—not only in a person but in an experience, idea, or object.

Each time you are introduced to a new person, listen to him. Each time you encounter a new experience, idea, or object, examine it. What about him—or it—do you really *like?* You should be able to find *at least* one thing that you can honestly approve of.

A Pattern for Change

Our American society as a whole could profit from

1. Greatly refined utilization of new and emerging audiovisual systems that make it feasible for us to see "instant replays" of crucial conversations, either staged or spontaneous. By reviewing, for instance, a vest-pocket summary of effective training he has undergone, a person should be able to assess his receptivity to unfamiliar ideas and people, to determine whether his behavior is nondefensive and his response warm, open, and meaningful.

2. Research aimed at discovering new ways of helping people etch out their "selfhood" as an important prelude to being able to reach out and *give* with confidence and sincerity.

3. Classroom facilities, in the various types of organizations where people must work together effectively, where groups of individuals can meet for critiques of each other's development as persons and as members of the team. If the man or woman being criticized is first asked to list all his strong and weak points as a human being and fellow worker *as he sees*

them, then he will resent less the comments made by his associates and will be better able to utilize them.

REFERENCE

1. "Youth and the Establishment: A Report on Research for John D. Rockefeller 3rd and the Task Force on Youth by Daniel Yankelovich Inc.," February 1, 1971, p. 71.

8

Competition and Candor

COMPETITION, we are told both here and abroad, is uniquely American. Without competition between groups and individuals, it is stoutly said, our free enterprise system would fold. Not only do we declare that competition is essential, but we consider it almost sacrosanct as a core element in our great (and potentially much greater) democracy. But is it all this? May it not be interfering, to some degree, with personal fulfillment and goal achievement? Let's take a closer look at it.

Amateur, Striver, or Pro?

Competition may be *expedient and self-defeating*, or it may be *tough and self-actualizing*. Depending upon the person involved and the way in which he views competition and is affected by it, the particular mixture of good and bad may vary markedly. Perhaps we might say that competition is never wholly good, never wholly bad. However, let's be more specific. Since competition is such an ever-present element in the American scene, let's discuss it in terms of three familiar personality types.

Type 1: The Amateur

A large corporation's executive vice-president once made this statement to his 18 key men in the course of a management seminar: "A top executive can be a 100 percent, unadulterated s.o.b., ruling his entire company by fear, but he is still a successful manager if his return on investment is in order."

What a tragic statement! And, regrettably, it reflects the kind of attitude—even though it is held by a small minority of executives—that all too many of our young people are thinking of when they disparage the business establishment.

This type of individual—whether he is an executive or not—we shall call the amateur. His principal thought in weighing any situation is: "What's in it for *me?* What can *I* get out of it?" He is the man who confirms the worst fears, the worst suspicions of the young person contemplating, or deciding to withdraw from, a career in business. This is particularly tragic because such an individual normally will not make nearly so significant an impact on his employer's corporate profit objectives as he might if he began to listen before telling; if he shifted from being a receiving set to being a transmitter—from implosive use of energy to explosive commitment to something bigger than self.

Type 2: The Striver

If the amateur, as we are saying in the context of this book, is an individual who perpetually drives himself to excel other people, who sees other organizations as direct threats to his own, the striver is the one who is always competing with his own potential, with his own dreams, with his own goals, with his own standards. Often he is simultaneously doing battle with real or imagined weaknesses in himself. Experiences of many kinds over the years have proved that this is the kind of person who keeps getting up and coming back after defeats and misfortunes that would be very disheartening to the amateur, whose only concern is to get the better of somebody else.

From birth a young man was slight of build and somewhat pigeon-breasted. While in junior high school, he ordered some body-building equipment and privately began lifting weights. He tried out for football only to break a leg. Then, as a high school sophomore, he developed an undiagnosed but extremely painful knee condition. Yet he persisted. He established time objectives for his track activities, attended summer basketball camp, and continued playing football. In spite of his pain he set the mile record in track for his particular school. Although he was ordered by his doctors to stay out of basketball for two years, and out of track for one year, as a senior he was a varsity starter on a winning football team and a state-champion relay-team member.

This young man competed with his own potential and acknowledged it to be his greatest challenger. He challenged himself academically, too—was a consistent honor student and was elected a member of the National Honor Society.

On the face of it, it could appear that we have described two extreme examples of competition in order to make a point. This is undoubtedly true. In the older, more mature group from which we selected our vice-president—the essence of the self-centered executive—we could also have found a great many fine, tough-minded executives who succeeded because they were always competing with that much more demanding thing called their own potential; because they shunned that more convenient competitor who lurked in the other guy. Similarly, other young men beset with the handicaps and bad luck of our ambitious athlete might have worn themselves out trying to beat that other guy without accepting the challenge of inner potential. They might even have shrunk from the physical pain and effort involved.

Dr. S. I. Hayakawa, the noted scholar and astute, gutsy president of San Francisco State College, cites the absurdity of raising large, healthy, muscular boys and young men and then abdicating the responsibility of giving them work and encouraging them in activities which will make them "tired and sweaty." In the absence of such effort, the expression of ennui through muscle cars, pot, unfocused protest, and the like can assume a disproportionately large priority in their lives. All too often, as a consequence, feelings of guilt or expedience begin to make themselves felt subliminally. These are eventually expressed through the classic defense mechanism of projection as these men put down those who represent vigor, work, confrontation, and achievement. (To them, of course, business can readily be considered the prime offender in this connection.)

The tendency to choose the much easier and more passive expedient of competing with the other guy can tell us much about the value system and future progress of any individual—and of a society.

Type 3: The Pro

In contrast even to the striver, who may be driven more by blind determination than by any plan for success, the pro competitor has a built-in system of stretching goals. This interpretation of the pro has been validated in conversations with champions from the sports world, with high-ranking business leaders, and with many others scarred by long lives of accomplishment.

In a family whose activities center strongly around equestrian show jumping, there were two sisters aged 12 and 18. The older girl had been asked to train and show a massive, energetic young horse who belonged to someone else. This horse had never been successfully shown because he was too strong and stubborn; he frequently would take the bit and go. After several months of intensive training, the girl felt this horse might be ready to show under the difficult, demanding conditions of jumping in the local charity horse show. One week before this show was to begin, however, she injured herself.

The younger sister had a suggestion. "Let me jump your horse," she said.

Turning to her father, the older girl asked in some wonderment, "What's the matter with this kid? Doesn't she realize that nobody has ever been able to collect and control this horse before?"

"Well," said Dad, "let's see what happens in the next few days."

After careful observation, it was determined that the sister should have her chance to ride and jump the horse during the first evening of the show. Any decision about the remaining three performances would be made afterward.

On the first evening, then, this girl who was barely 12 years old took her own jumping horse—a mare—into the arena. After she had completed three jumps, she suddenly found the horse refusing the next one. A moment later she flew over the mare's head and landed on the obstacles. The ringmaster immediately called for an ambulance; and, while the father was making his way from the opposite end of the arena where the girls always asked him to stand, he could hear voices murmuring, "The little girl seems to be badly hurt."

Suddenly, a clear voice rang out: "Out of my way! I've got a horse to ride!"

Back came the youngster through the crowd—not on her own horse but on the big, traditionally uncontrollable Palomino. She went into the ring again before anybody could stop her and took a beautiful round, skimming over the jumps with a grace and courage that brought the onlookers to their feet with a roar. As she came riding out, her father—with tears in his eyes—said, "Honey, I don't know how we're going to be able to afford him, but you just earned yourself a horse!"

The point? No matter what the age, no matter what the title or lack thereof, there is always room and a need for anyone whose attitude is truly that of a pro.

The older of these two sisters, incidentally, had a significant conversation with her father when she was 16. He was suggesting exuberantly that, with her new horse, she could possibly beat a well-known member of the equestrian team in a forthcoming show. The girl seemed puzzled; in an almost reproving tone she said, "Dad, I don't want to beat *her*. I want to *win*, if I can, so that people will know my training methods are that good and my horse is that good. I think I would have given up jumping after my second or third trip to the hospital if I wasn't competing with *me*."

How can we apply this philosophy to a typical superior/subordinate situation? All too often the so-called mature manager misses some splendid opportunities to help young subordinates perceive, develop, and utilize new skills, new strengths, new insights. He seldom acknowledges that they could make a substantially greater contribution to organizational objectives. Why? Because he sees them as competitors.

We submit that the manager who is a pro is truly interested in the future of his young subordinates and that he places a premium on example—on constantly and systematically increasing the effectiveness of the man he displays to those subordinates every morning as he arrives at work. He is competing with his own potential, and he knows that the total value of what he has to display each day is the sum of the values between his ears. If these are amateur values, his leadership and results will be amateurish. If he is merely an instinctive striver, they may still fall short. But if he has pro values, he'll function and produce like a pro.

What You Want: Is It Bigger Than You?

"You know, I think we're a dying breed." So said yet another student who is working his way through school. Conversation with him revealed an impassioned soul filled with sadness for those individuals who "smoke," feel a need to tell people off and put people down, or drink a lot for that extra confidence. He referred to a comment in *The New York Times:*

> Young people, not having to fear for tomorrow, lack the necessity to fight for their existence, and this gives rise to a situation in which they face no problems that require their strength and will. . . . All this taken together deprives the life of young people of any permanent substance. . . . Different forms of narcotics, which are more and more common among young people as a way of escaping reality, of course, provide only temporary escape. But, as is known, they lead to a breakdown in the nervous system and deepen a depression.[1]

This young man talked at length about the minority of students who are facing up to the challenges before them in the 1970s. The prevailing reaction among the majority to working 40 hours a week and also being successful full-time students, he agreed, can only be called *fear:* fear of *responsibility,* fear of *failing,* fear of *discouragement,* fear of *self.* Why not replace those frightening phrases, he suggested, with others concerned with ideas, goals, individual values, self-appreciation?

Strange ideas to hear from a young man, perhaps—though not if the groups he runs around with are moving in a downbeat, unhappy circuit. And approximately 92 percent of the 560 people in his graduating class, this student said, were *at least* smoking pot and in many cases dropping acid.

What is the trouble with such young people—those who are so unhappy now that they are in college or otherwise on their own? Apparently they were "hassled," not guided, in their earlier years. They were:

1. Told, not asked.
2. Talked *at,* not *with.*
3. Undisciplined. (The Webster definition of "discipline" is "that which builds, strengthens, and molds.")
4. Conditioned to avoid confronting difficulties.
5. Criticized excessively.

As a result, self-hatred took over when their problems multiplied and the very parents who created them began to distrust them and—it seemed—stopped loving them.

Take the simple matter of responsibility. If a parent fails to expect any, the typical child will naturally assume none. Often, the child feels guilty as he matures and—with no responsibility for his own well-being, either physical or mental—still must depend upon his parent's financial support to finish school. To appease his conscience, he then resorts to hating and criticizing himself. Discontented, worried about the predicament in which he finds himself, he finally strikes back at life by hating other people. His parents, then, are often convenient symbols toward whom he projects his self-loathing.

In a newspaper article, Sydney Harris describes what he terms today's "anti-people." These are the people who hate, fear, destroy, and have forgotten how to love.

> As you know, one of the great cosmic discoveries of our century has been "anti-matter." It has been found that every atomic particle in the universe has its "anti-matter" counterpart—a sort of mirror-image.
>
> Matter and anti-matter are opposite in electric charge, but identical in mass. And if the two should ever collide, both will immediately blow up and disappear.
>
> On bleak days, when I look at the headlines from all over the world and shudder, I am tempted to engage in the

philosophical conceit that we are not really "people" at all. We are "anti-people."

It really makes more sense that way. Somewhere in the universe there are real "people." They are the positive charge, of which we are the negative. They have the same mass, and look just like us; but they have prudently avoided us for millions of years, knowing that if they came into contact with "anti-people" we would all blow up.

Dimly we perceive what positively charged people would be like. We have had a few specimens—not many—throughout the ages. They are people in whom love dominates hate, intelligence controls impulse, joy conquers bitterness, cooperation wins over rivalry. They live each for all and all for each.

We are the mirror-image, the "anti-people" of the universe. We are divided by politics, by nation, by race, by sex, by religion, by ideology, by the most idiotic of beliefs, prejudices and superstitions. Time and again, we kill off millions of our bravest and our best for reasons we can hardly comprehend a few years afterwards.

No other species that behaved so irrationally and so self-destructively could possibly survive long anywhere in the universe. Our conduct is contrary to all the laws of nature, reason and our own revealed religion. We are supremely unable to practice what we love being preached about; we want everyone else to start acting better before we will take that perilous chance.

Is this not the definition of "anti-people" more than of "people"? Are we not what "human beings" ought to be, but turned inside out, with our vices perpetually trampling our virtues? Do we not use our knowledge more for greed and vanity than for goodness; use our passions more for extermination than for reconciliation; use our lofty principles more for camouflage than for conformance?

The galaxies, we are told, are receding further away from us at incredible speeds. Who can blame them? And who can

> doubt that on some distant planet, the real "people" are
> breathing a sigh of relief that their chances of colliding with
> us grow remoter every day? [2]

Perhaps the tone of this article is unduly pessimistic. Perhaps the writer has reason to be pessimistic. But it's not too late to change the negativism implied. The situation might just reverse itself if enough happy "real people" said to enough unhappy anti-people, in effect, "Try to follow in our footsteps. Then, together, we can get moving and go places!"

Expediency Is Out of Date

There are some typical patterns of activity and performance which characterize the expedient and self-defeating competitor on the one hand and the tough and self-actualizing competitor on the other.

Expedient and Self-defeating	Tough and Self-actualizing
Idleness	Work
Avoidance of difficulty	Confrontation
No competitive spark	Competition with self
Purposelessness	Purposefulness; stretching goals
Hate	Love
Self-deception	Truth
Despair; nihilism	Faith and hope
Sarcasm	Compassion
Calculated defensiveness	Calculated "openness," even vulnerability

The self-defeating individual asks, "What can I *get?*" The self-actualizer asks, "What can I *give?*"

You see, we really don't have to compete with ourselves at all as long as we can convince ourselves that life "out there" is not very good or very promising. But this kind of pessimism and expediency is now out of date. The syndicated columnist Nick Thimmesch recently headed a piece "Fed Up with Doomsday Doctrines?" In it he said:

> There are encouraging signs that people are fed up with the pessimism inflicted on us by the influential doomsday claque over the environment, race relations, Vietnam, the generation gap and the economy. . . . Now it's time to break with this interlude of despair. Just as it is foolhardy to believe that life automatically gets better, that wrongs are righted by computer, or that guardian angels always steer us safely, it is equally a mistake to forget that we have free will to meet many challenges, and to assume that all is lost.[3]

A Pattern for Change

Maslow's perceptive, competent studies of peak experiences and self-actualization have revealed that man is fundamentally good and is capable, potentially, of greatness. It is time that massive sums of money were allocated by concerned organizations and individuals—whether patriotic, idealistic, or pragmatic (is there really a difference in this context?)—to study and apply further the existing findings in our three key areas:

1. Self-discovery
2. Self-fulfillment
3. Self-actualization

The potential role of the individual who sees his opportunities and commitments as inexhaustible is staggering. It can also be wonderfully exciting. Think of the worldwide scope of the top corporation executive, or the dedicated statesman, in times like ours. If, however, you are a present or potential leader who doesn't really like himself—who is weakness- rather than strength-oriented— you may close this book in disdain (or *fear?*) after reading the challenge inherent in these words.

REFERENCES

1. *The New York Times,* August 2, 1971. © 1971 by The New York Times Company. Reprinted by permission.
2. Sydney J. Harris, "Somewhere There Are Real People," *Chicago Daily News,* July 30, 1971. Reprinted by permission of Sydney J. Harris and Publishers-Hall Syndicate.
3. Nick Thimmesch, "Fed Up with Doomsday Doctrines?" *Des Moines Register,* September 17, 1971. Copyright, 1971, Los Angeles Times. Reprinted with permission.

9

Drugs: Where Do You Get Your "High"?

THE self-actualized person gets his "high" from setting a goal, overcoming the obstacles in the way of his getting there, and finally reaching the goal only to set another one further ahead. The self-defeating person, on the other hand, the one who refuses to set goals and face up to difficulties, whose aimless existence is guided only by expediency, often finds a cop-out in drugs.

Here are two distinct "options," strictly incompatible. The first is hard drugs; the second, in contrast, is hard, toughening experience. Let's examine them both.

The Sudden Realization

To paraphrase a well-known quotation from *Raisin in the Sun*—"What happens to a crisis deferred?" What happens when the young and the not-so-young begin to realize that they've never really faced *anything*—anything tough, that is? Anything that requires them to reach—no, not for a cocktail or a pill—but deep inside themselves for new resources, new fiber, new toughness?

Both behavioral science research and empirical observation suggest that individuals in this predicament can turn to drugs if they are suddenly encouraged, or forced, to make tough decisions or face sticky, messy confrontations. Their trouble is that they have not, in the past, experienced a steady build-up of difficult or mind-toughening situations.

Fran, a 16-year-old, learned at close range about the drug-abuse problem in her high school. She had chosen to spend her summer days working in the local Woolworth's to earn money for her college fund. When a couple of her girl friends asked why they hadn't been able to reach her over the phone, she said lightly, "Well, I've been keeping pretty busy. What have you been up to?" The replies she received were similar to a great many responses from teenagers all over the nation to the same question: goofing off, dating, sleeping late, messing around, "Oh, nothing much!"—just being bored or getting ready to go back to school.

Quite a contrast! One girl was able to get rid of her frustrations by working hard and learning to appreciate many new people of different ages, personalities, and ways of life. Her friends, on the other hand, became increasingly tired from lack of responsibility and challenge.

One friend, Jean, accompanied her on a short trip before school reopened in September. It soon became obvious that the friend, who had smoked marijuana for some time, had recently begun to experiment with stronger drugs. The two girls argued all during the trip, the one wanting to find a source for the drugs she needed more and more, the other just wanting to swim and enjoy the mountains. Finally, Jean found a supply of pot. Fran told her, "Look! I don't care if you smoke—as long as you really want to. But it's stupid! *You're* stupid, and you can forget about my ever taking another trip with you."

Such strong words from a girl she had admired for her ambition and popularity hurt Jean, and the two girls parted silently. Neither knew that Fran's outburst would be the catalyst for Jean's eventual recovery. But a month later Fran received a phone call from a girl who identified herself as Jean. At first Fran didn't recognize the voice because it held some of its old sparkle.

Jean said haltingly, "I guess I've found out who my *real* friend is. You were frank enough to tell me I was acting like an idiot. I figured you were just dull, but now it hurts when I remember how we broke up, Fran, and I've thought a lot about your last words to me. Anyway, I've quit the drug bit and am trying to make some new friends. If I don't see you any more, thanks just the same."

Fran hopes Jean was telling the truth. "You know," she said, "I'm lucky to have had parents who loved me but set me an example of honest work and told me that if if I wanted 'extras' and new clothes I'd have to work. It makes me tired—even mad—sometimes, when customers are unreasonable, but it helps me keep my head on straight." And so, in a few short sentences, she illustrated what so many parents (and supervisors) need to remember. Don't make it so easy on your kids (or subordinates). Delegate some responsibility to them. Help them find challenges to face head-on and overcome. *Love* them enough to do this!

Beyond the Night

Any reader who has participated in a typical management/youth symposium may well recognize certain aspects of the scene on which we shall now focus.

This particular symposium has been set up with the idea that each of four representatives of management and each of four members of a youth group from selected campuses will make a five-minute initial presentation. One of this latter group is a young man whose hair hangs down to his shoulders, whose mustache droops over his mouth, who is thin virtually to the point of emaciation.

This young man's opening remark is, "I am an anarchist." As the three-hour exchange between the managers and the young people unfolds, this young man keeps up a commentary which at least seems to strike a consistent note. That is, it is redolent with uncompromising statements of a tedious sameness: "All businessmen are ruthless." "Business is just no damned good." "We've got to bring the whole system tumbling down around us." "All businessmen are full of s--t." "The future is black, and there is no alternative to anarchy." And so on—*ad infinitum, ad nauseam, ad myopiam.*

When asked whether or not he believed in dreams, stretching objectives, trying to live up to the future potential of a great country in a world of potential greatness, the young man becomes increasingly sullen. "Words like that are embarrassing," he says. And then, sarcastically, "Don't you get the message that there is no hope for man? That man is fundamentally no damned good?"

The more this young fellow is urged to discuss the somewhat overworked phrase "the light at the end of the tunnel," the more he seems obsessed with immersing himself in his own conception of an endless night. Why? Why does he prefer wallowing in self-pity, despair, and corrosive dissent? Because it helps him avoid *work, change, growth, effort.* His condition of poor physical and mental health seems to have cemented him into a vicious circle.

This is too bad. With a little exposure to work, change, growth, and effort, he might learn to like and respect himself. Perhaps, then, he might someday swell the ranks— where he is badly needed—of ambitious, energetic, upstanding managers of enterprise. *Fortune* might even be able to quote him as it quotes other, more percipient young men's remarks about their organizations and their jobs:

> ". . . While here, you have guys that are really fabulous, so the competition is *a little tougher.* But it is a lot more stimulating atmosphere." [Italics ours.]

> "I prefer a job with *high risk* and the possibility of rapid advancement." [Italics ours.]

> "Around here they give you all the responsibility you can handle and all the rope you need to hang yourself—it's very exciting."

"Junior managers," *Fortune* declares, "want to operate *on their own* without someone peering over their shoulder. They crave autonomy." Again: "Possessed of a deep faith in social change, the junior manager is quite willing to debate his superiors on matters of basic ideology." [1] And Chairman Irwin Miller of Cummins Engines, pioneers in job enrichment, is reported as saying:

> We have to pay serious, dignified attention to individuals. We will stand or fall on how we handle this. The ethic of

the young is to contribute. The best way to keep the ablest of the young people is to load them up a little beyond their capacity. That capacity then turns out to be very high.[2]

This last strikes right to the heart of the matter. It explains so much that needs to be understood about how to eliminate the ennui and self-loathing that lead straight into the quicksand of drug dependency.

A young fellow on campus was expressing real chagrin about his apparent inability to grow long, luxuriant whiskers, mustache, and sideburns. "Why is this so important to you?" he was asked. The answer might be considered revealing and even startling. "If I had all that to hide behind," he said, "nobody would be able to tell when I'm frightened or when I'm sad. Nobody would be able to see what a victim I am of circumstances over which I have no control. I wouldn't have to measure up to the demands of people who really couldn't care less whether I live or die. Oh, Lord, if I was just in charge of something— at least *me*—I wouldn't *need* to hide."

Now, what had induced this young man to wallow in such an excess of self-loathing? For one thing, he'd probably never felt the satisfaction that comes from making a contribution, however small, to a truly worthwhile cause.

Great Things Begin with Great Dreams

The pretty young stewardess, literally glowing with health and enthusiasm, said: "I have this friend who's just out of law school. He wants to prove he has courage, so he's turned down this position with a big law firm and is getting into drugs. He feels he must attack this problem even though he'll probably get hooked. But he's just got to get away from the artificial, inhuman, plastic world." She added, "I know he's not doing the right thing, but I don't know what to tell him."

Just another sad, wan paradox of the type that is so characteristic of a frequently paradoxical and anachronistic generation. This young man's device for "attacking" (succumbing to?) drugs was to consume substances which perfectly embody words like "artificial," "synthetic," "inhuman," "plastic," and so forth. To conquer evil, he was prepared to nourish it.

If we were to follow this young man's example, to find the light, we would seek the darkness. To toughen our minds we would seek mind-softening chemicals. How vital it is becoming to unmask many of the currently modish words for what they are—and small wonder! "Attack," in this instance, was really "retreat."

The willingness to face today's fashionable terms and concepts for what they are. The courage to dream and put muscle into those dreams—to set objectives, develop timetables, accept individual accountability, become deeply involved in something (not a pill or a needle) bigger than self—this is the stuff of tomorrow's relevant person.

Let's (dare we say it once more?) tell it like it is!

A Pattern for Change

We must begin to undergird the plethora of superficial efforts now being addressed to the solution of drug problems by driving to the heart of the human condition: the need for *purpose* and *meaning* in our lives—for hard work and stern tests, for love and self-actualization. Are you fully familiar with all the organizations in your community whose purpose it is to eliminate drug abuse?

REFERENCES

1. Judson Gooding, "The Accelerated Generation Moves into Management," *Fortune* (March 1971). Used by permission.
2. Irwin Miller, "The Accelerated Generation Gap," *Fortune* (March 1971). Used by permission.

10

The Builders
and the Bores

ACCORDING to the laws of cybernetics, the results you can expect from a project or an endeavor are in direct proportion to what you have contributed to it.

As computer specialists say rather crudely, "Garbage in, garbage out." They mean that if you superimpose a costly computer and data processing system on inefficient procedures and indifferent employees, the results will be no better than you deserve. The printout, no matter how imposing, will be worthless.

There is something here of Christ's admonition: "As ye reap . . ." We are even reminded of the Golden Rule: "As ye would that men should do to you, do ye also to them likewise." Again, each receives back according to his contribution.

In an infinite variety of ways we continue to verify this

truth. For instance, people like to feel good about themselves, about their accomplishments to date and their potential for still greater things, but they will feel good only if what you tell them in an effort to make them think or act the way you want them to is the truth and is consistent, as they see it, with what you yourself believe and do. It must be obvious that you are *really* telling it like it is! In short, for the desired results the input must be right. If you as a manager want hard, conscientious work, *you* must be a hard, conscientious worker. If you are a parent and expect your son or daughter to shun drugs, you must successfully resist your own particular antidote to boredom and frustration—whether it is alcohol or whatever.

And so we say in the context of this chapter: If you are a *bore* you will encounter many bores. If you are a *builder,* you will encounter many builders.

We Make Our Own Climate

At a party, one guest approached another. "Isn't this whole thing a bore?" the first man asked. And the second retorted, "Yes! *You* are!"

In contrast, just listen to this statement from a flier in love with his life and his work: "When there's no ground visibility, just rain and smoggy fog, and I have to take off with only instruments, there is no greater experience than breaking through the clouds to face the sun all over the heavens."

Is this simply a pungent little comparison? Not really. We do much to create the immediate climate in which we find ourselves. The title of this chapter is no idle juxtaposition of words. We ask the reader, regardless of age, "Are you a builder or a bore?" The implications of this question are identical for each of us.

Suppose, for instance, that through some marvelous spiritual alchemy, all the members of your family or your organizational unit (or the nation) were to practice being builders for 72 hours. The possibilities stagger the imagination!

Is it a question of *what* will work? Or how much we want to *make* it work?

Why Be Boring?

This is the president of a sizable company speaking: "We've had a company creed—you might call it a philosophy—for three years now, and I can't really see that anything significant has happened. I thought a company creed was supposed to make such a contribution to a profitable business."

When his firm's creed was examined, it was clear that the words, the phrasing, the whole context might be summed up in the following list of adjectives: bland, pedantic, paternalistic, patronizing, smug, dull, dreary. Yet the basic purpose of a philosophy or creed should be to provide stretch, a feeling of purpose, guidance—and, yes, inspiration (the spirit within). Perhaps, too, from a motivational standpoint it should provide—above all—the basis, the ingredients, for a sense of identification with something *bigger than self* on the part of the individual member of the working team.

One wearies of the seeming fear or reluctance on the part of a great many management people to write or to issue any kind of statement filled with crisp, sparkling, zestful, emotion-tinged words. They seem to worry lest, somehow, management be branded as "square" or "believers in apple pie and motherhood." This is an immature attitude if there ever was one.

Why must we be bores? Why do we need to make a philosophy sound dull? Why load it with pallid, shuffling, slogging words? (Let's have a "dialogue.") In turning out such an unattractive product, we overlook the opportunity to introduce some key climate-building thoughts, issue new challenges, even sound a clarion call to identification with something good and important.

If *you yourself* do not feel that the function of your department, division, company, home, or self is that good, then you know where to start.

Let's Grow Up—and Start Acting Like Children

One of the most powerfully effective and joyful things that any adult can do is to feel and communicate a sense of wonder. The jaded, disdain-filled sophisticate is usually the victim of a self-manufactured malaise of the spirit— the cool, fashionable purveyor of retreat.

This malaise takes the thrust and meaning and fun out of life. And so we find ourselves echoing a phrase that has gained some popularity lately: "Why don't we grow up and start acting like children?" Indeed, if we are going to look at the world with eyes of wonder, walking around with calculated vulnerability, with our defenses down, drinking in all that is good and worthwhile and potent and challenging about us, then we might very well emulate the young child who has not yet decided that life is a defensive, losing, cynical endeavor.

Here, perhaps, is the best place to talk about the book which is currently exploiting and prostituting our latent dreams—the "child of wonder left behind," the often frustrated yearnings of a society beset with problems of ecology, man's inhumanity toward man and all its dolorous ramifications. (Of course, we must never lose the capacity to dream, but a dream deferred because of work deferred becomes an ultimate horror—an albatross, a nightmare.) The author in question is Charles Reich, and the book is *The Greening of America*.

In this book, Reich plays on our dreams and desires, our longing for warmth, love, beauty, truth, and spontaneity. He offers a way "forward," a "better" way—a series of passive placebos. But we'd like to propose a simple response to be applied to every idyllic palliative he puts forth. This is the question or series of questions:

Who will do the *work?*
When will there be time for *work?*
How will you make it *work?*
Where will the *workers* come from?

Why are we concerned about this book? Why, indeed? Dozens, hundreds, perhaps thousands of readers—executives and aspiring executives among them—protest: "I never even finished it. I couldn't." However, tens of thousands of highly impressionable young people *have* finished it.

Reich proclaims the joys of uninhibited youth, which he sees in images such as pulsing to music, taking delight in raunchiness, playing, laughing—he takes comfort when they "flare against authority." But they are doomed in his vision, victims of "Squarestown." He sees them soon in a lifeless condition, "their minds lobotomized," in the "windowless, endless corridors of the Corporate State." [1]

One who has walked down countless corporate corridors and known innumerable corporations and individuals may be entitled to wonder if Reich is living in and talking about the same country the rest of us know and love. Faults, yes! Problems, yes! Aching needs, yes! We submit, however, that fleeing behind a cloud of pot smoke and freaking out in various ways is not the answer. Groping for self through the casting aside of all inhibition is not the answer. What is the answer—or an important element in it—is a perpetual sense of wonder.

Identification with Quality

The search is for self, for individuality. The surest road to success here, as we have said, is *work:* objectives, tasks, confrontations, difficulties, building, growth, self-knowledge. And identification with something truly worthy of our best efforts.

For there is a strong need in all of us to identify with something or someone—a need which may be more and more difficult to satisfy these days, particularly among the young. Finding No. 34 of *Youth and the Establishment*, the Yankelovich report on research for John D. Rockefeller 3rd, reads:

> The identification of college youth with other students has become more pervasive, while identification with other groups including other young people, the middle class, people of the same nationality and religion has declined over the past year. The one exception is the family where student ties and relations remain strong.[2]

Our challenge: Do you have the courage, do you have the desire, to accumulate and synthesize a value system that makes it unnecessary for you to "identify" with any particular group? Which, rather, enables you to identify on the basis of quality of ideas—intrinsic or innate ideas— with other people regardless of age, regardless of type, regardless of caste, regardless of class, regardless of anything except excellence of mind and soul expressed through example? End of challenge.

Find Yourself by Losing Yourself . . .

It has been the privilege of the senior member of this author team to have led many seminars throughout the United States—indeed, over much of the world that is not behind the Iron Curtain—discussing time and again the patterns of leadership conclusively demonstrated by the great leaders of history. When the seminar participants are asked to name great leaders, the roster always includes five men (in order of recency): Sir Winston Churchill, Mahatma Gandhi, Julius Caesar, Jesus (again the historical Jesus, not the Christ), and Socrates. And, among the powerful, virtually ageless statements attributed to these much admired leaders, we find many mind-stretching exhortations to their followers: calls for sacrifice, admonitions suggesting that example has indeed proved to be the most trusted and effective method of leadership. The principle of high expectations is wonderfully typified, also—for instance, in these words of Gandhi: "You will find yourself by losing yourself in service to your fellowman, your country, and your God." This statement also speaks beautifully to the perpetual question of the Existentialist who keeps asking: "Who am I?"

The stature of these leaders is validated by history, by the implacable, objective phenomenon called *results achievement.* The extent to which they and their followers accomplished great things through stretching, often painful and traumatic, experiences has made inspiring reading down through the years. Yet, for some reason, the average leader of a business, a university, or a government unit seems to shy away from using their kind of pulse-quickening and imaginative phrases. What a mistake!

Organizations of all kinds remain only the assortment of brick, steel, and mortar that houses them unless they are moved by the vital thing called inspiration or "spirit within" in action. Appeals to reason, apart from the emotions, of course have their uses, but must the one rule out the other? Should we not be able to link reason with inspiration? The first need not and does not always precede the second in any precise and predictable way. Each must nourish and support the other, or real results simply will not materialize. The fully functioning individual, the *actualized personality,* knows he needs both reason and inspiration.

A Force That "Drives and Guides"

In Communism, which is viewed by so many as perhaps the greatest threat to our free American way of life, the power of losing oneself in a common endeavor has long been understood. Whatever else we may say about the dedicated Communist, he doesn't lack enthusiasm and devotion to his cause—enthusiasm and devotion that, in many cases, have been inspired by leaders who know the price of words.

Let's examine carefully two paragraphs written by a former Eastern university student who had gone to Mexico and there become a Communist. These paragraphs are taken from a letter he wrote to his fiancée breaking their engagement:

> We Communists have a high casualty rate. We are the ones who get shot and hung and lynched and tarred and feathered and jailed and slandered and fired from our jobs, and in every other way made as uncomfortable as possible. A certain percentage of us get killed or imprisoned. We live in virtual poverty. We turn back to the party every penny we make above what is absolutely necessary to keep alive. We Communists don't have the time or the money for any movies or concerts or T-Bone steaks or decent homes or new cars. We've been described as fanatics. We are fanatics, our lives are dominated by one great overshadowing factor—the struggle for world Communism. We Communists have a philosophy of life which no amount of money could buy.
>
> We have a cause to fight for, a definite purpose in life; we subordinate our petty personal selves into a great movement of humanity, and if our personal lives seem hard or our egos appear to suffer through subordination to the party, then we are adequately compensated by the thought that each of us in his small way is contributing to something new and true and better for mankind.
>
> There is one thing about which I am in dead earnest, and that is the Communist cause. It is my life, my business, my religion, my hobby, my sweetheart, my wife and mistress, my bread and my meat. I work at it in the daytime and dream of it at night. Its hold on me grows, not lessens, as time goes on. Therefore, I cannot carry on a friendship, a love affair, or even a conversation, without relating it to this force

which both drives and guides my life. I evaluate people, books, ideas and actions according to how they affect the Communist cause and by their attitude toward it. I have already been in jail because of my ideas and, if necessary, I am ready to go before a firing squad.

We may disagree strongly with the source of this man's motivation, but his words are definitely not boring to read.

For Dedicated Effort . . . to Greatness

Isn't it ironic that, in gatherings of important, successful executives in posh watering spots all over America, we constantly hear real concern expressed about better communication, not only with young people but with the not-so-young as well? About the need for encouraging some commitment, some real motivation to achieve corporate and other organizational objectives? But, almost to a man, these leaders hesitate to issue the kind of strong, powerful call (framed in crunchy, juicy words) that will stir people to dedicated effort, that will appeal to the deep craving for feelings of significance, contribution, and identification with big things which is the heart and soul of human nature.

We have alluded to this strange hesitancy before, but it is worth asking the question again: Why the seeming fear of evocative, mind-stretching, and even emotional words and phrases? Whatever the reason for it, it must be overcome: *A true leader cannot be afraid to stand out from the crowd, to espouse new ideas and causes before they are taken up by the average person, to promote and defend them eloquently.*

Consider for a moment, in this context, the following statement of John W. Gardner, former Secretary of Health, Education and Welfare and now head of Common Cause:

> Back of every great civilization, behind all the panoply of power and wealth, is something as powerful as it is insubstantial; a set of ideas, attitudes and convictions—and the confidence that those ideas and convictions are viable. No nation can achieve greatness unless it believes in something, and unless that something has the moral dimensions to sustain a great civilization. If the *light of belief* [italics ours] flickers out, then all the productive capacity and all the know-how and all the power of the nation will be as nothing and the darkness will gather.[3]

And here is another by Thomas J. Watson, Jr., board chairman of the IBM Corporation:

> Strangely, the expounders of many of the great new ideas of history were frequently considered on the lunatic fringe for some or all of their lives. If one stands up and is counted from time to time, one may get knocked down, but remember this: A man flattened by an opponent can get up again. A man flattened by conformity stays down for good.[4]

Crawford R. Greenawalt, of Du Pont, says:

> Behind every advance of the human race is a germ of creation growing in the mind of some lone individual whose dreams waken him in the night while others lie contentedly asleep. It is he who is the indispensable man.[5]

Hence this further challenge to the reader, regardless of age—and let's hope the spectrum is broad. *Find yourself by losing yourself* in commitment to strong, stretching, powerful, tough ideas. As a member of your particular generation, begin to communicate on the basis of ideas bigger than you are. This will have the effect of routing out defensiveness and other negative reactions which, often, simply stultify communication and preclude the blending of effort toward the achievement of good, practical, greatly to be desired goals.

A Pattern for Change

1. Make it a point to challenge the bored hypersophisticate, whether young or not so young, to cease the retreat from what he probably calls priggish moralizing. Perhaps we have no real problem in our society today which would remain significant if we would rigorously and vigorously "wholesomize" our moral climate. The doubters should, in the interest of intellectualism in the best sense of the word, be cajoled, wheedled, or dared to undergo the agonizing mental experience of *doubting their doubts*. This is tough! But it tends to separate the pseudo- or quasi-intellectual from the individual who has real intellectual commitment, staying power, and integrity.

2. Advocate properly funded and carefully organized research to probe the moral viscera of our society in order to determine what kinds of nourishment are needed: the source, the method, the process. Have you read any sociology texts on social disorganization lately? If so, what did you learn the most about? *Building* or *destruction?* This, too, must change. To quote the poet Edwin Markham:

> We are all blind until we see
> That in the human plan
> Nothing is worth the making if
> It does not make the man.

Why build these cities glorious
If man unbuilded goes?
In vain we build a world, unless
The builder also grows.[6]

Decide that you want to believe in something beautiful and strive to see that beauty in each day and
event in your life.

REFERENCES

1. Charles Reich, *The Greening of America* (New York: Random House, 1970).
2. "Youth and the Establishment: A Report on Research for John D. Rockefeller 3rd and the Task Force on Youth by Daniel Yankelovich Inc.," February 1, 1971, p. 73.
3. John W. Gardner, *Excellence* (New York: Harper & Row, 1961).
4. Thomas J. Watson, Jr., *A Business and Its Beliefs* (New York: McGraw-Hill, 1963).
5. Crawford R. Greenawalt, *The Uncommon Man* (New York: McGraw-Hill, 1959).
6. Edwin Markham, untitled poem, in *One Thousand Quotable Poems,* edited by Thomas Clark (New York: Clark & Co., 1937).

11

Four Deadly Words

THERE are certain overworked words and phrases that definitely imply an unwillingness to come to grips with life, face up to problems, *do* things. "Precedent," "establishment," and "they" are in this category. Another example is "dialogue." Some eyebrows may shoot up when we include this last very faddish and moddish term as smacking of expediency or copping out; however, the faithful reader of this book will have noted a certain prejudice against it.

The Power of Anger

The following episode took place on the eighth floor of a large department store in Montreal. One man stepped out of the elevator and immediately was hailed by another. "You old so-and-so, you knew what you were doing, didn't you?" "I don't know what you're talking about. In fact, I don't even believe we've met," said the first man.

The other grinned. "No," he said, "of course you wouldn't remember me—I was just a member of the audience the last time you were up here for that management seminar, several months ago, and you gave us that big challenge."

Feeling that he would find out sooner or later what the challenge was all about, the visitor asked politely, "And what have you been doing since then?"

The Montrealer's only reply was to repeat his opening sally: "You knew what you were doing, didn't you?"

"What do you mean?"

"Well," said the first man, "you told us you suspected that a good many of us probably didn't have the guts to get ourselves into the kind of top physical condition that we were capable of, consistent with our doctor's approval. You made me so sore I made up my mind to show you. That night at home I set the clock for five o'clock. I was going to get up and do some jogging—" (This was before jogging had become a popular pastime.) "—but as I walked out on the street it was chilly and dark and I had the acute feeling that everybody up and down the block was peering at me from behind the blinds. I almost went back into the house and chucked the whole thing. This fear of subjecting myself to talk and ridicule was the main reason I had never taken up jogging before, even though I really yearned to get in better physical condition. But I remembered your words and they made me mad all over again.

"So," the man continued, "I took off. I jogged and I walked, and I jogged and I jogged and I jogged, and finally I came back, took a shower, ate breakfast, and went to work. At first I felt just great. Then, about three hours later,

I was so groggy I almost fell asleep at my desk. I barely got through the day. The next morning I again set the alarm for five o'clock and had an even more difficult time getting out of bed. The only thing that kept me going was your challenge. Once more, as I walked out that morning, I just about turned and went back in because I wondered what on earth the neighbors would be thinking.

"However," said the Montrealer, "I kept it up, and each time I began to like it just a little bit more and hate it just a little bit less. On the fifth morning—to my surprise —my neighbor across the street came trotting out in sweat clothes. 'Mind if I join you?' he called." Then the Montreal man looked at the out-of-towner with that characteristic sparkle in his eye and said once again, "You old so-and-so, you knew what you were doing, didn't you?"

By the end of two weeks five people from the neighborhood had asked to join the early-morning joggers. And now, three months later, the group totaled thirteen. They were making plans to meet once a month in order to discuss ways in which they could increase not only their physical but also their mental tone.

The first man reached over and grabbed the second by the arm with what can only be described as a viselike grip. "You old so-and-so, you sure made me sore, but I'm sure glad you did." And he walked off chuckling.

The Frustrating Four

What implications does this little story have for the four words that we have cited as being deadly in their potential? It illustrates how each in its own way frustrates innovation, individuality, and high achievement.

Precedent

Sam Walter Foss has written a poem, *The Calf Path,* in which he tells how a rough track through the woods was made by a homing calf and, over the years, was followed by a dog, a flock of sheep, and in time—crooked though it was—by men who "wound in and out, /And dodged and turned and bent about, and uttered words of righteous wrath." The path became a lane, a road, a village street, a city thoroughfare.

> Each day a hundred thousand men, followed this zig-zag calf again,
> And o'er his crooked journey went, the traffic of a continent.
> A hundred thousand men were led, by one calf near three centuries dead.
> They followed still his crooked way, and lost one hundred years a day;
> For thus such reverence is lent, to a well-established precedent.

For, says the poet,

> . . . men are prone to go it blind, along the calf path of the mind,
> And work away from sun to sun, to do what other men have done.
> They follow in the beaten track, and in and out, and forth and back.
> And still their devious course pursue, to keep the path that others do.
>
> They keep the path a sacred groove, along which all their lives they move;

> But how the old wood-gods laugh, who first saw the
> primeval calf . . . .

So much for this bit of folk wisdom. On a more sophisticated level we have the warning of historian Arnold
Toynbee:

> Of the twenty-two civilizations that appear in history, nine-
> teen of them collapsed when they reached the moral state
> the United States is in now. The average age of the world's
> great civilizations has been 200 years. All nations have pro-
> gressed through this sequence:
>
>   From bondage to spiritual faith
>   From spiritual faith to great courage
>   From courage to liberty
>   From liberty to abundance
>   From abundance to selfishness
>   From selfishness to complacency
>   From complacency to *apathy* [italics ours]
>   From apathy to dependency
>   From dependency back again into bondage.

It is of course apathy—ignorance of, or flight from, our
strength—that makes us cling to precedent. Need we say
more?

The Establishment

An audience of 2,000 managers recently was asked:
"Suppose you were given five minutes to write down your
careful definition of 'the Establishment.' How many different definitions would there be?" And the answer came back
with a roar: "Two thousand!"

If we accept the truism that beauty is in the eye of the
beholder, perhaps we can also say that "the Establishment"

118

is in the eye of the beholder. Clearly, the phrase can mean just about anything we want it to. And, if we want to avoid change, innovation, confrontation, growth, awareness, and continuous new self-actualization, we are certainly helped in our endeavor by making frequent and imaginative use of the term "the Establishment." It is relatively easy—a passive expedient—to assume consistently that something of the sort is lurking "out there somewhere," intent upon thwarting us. And the prevalent vogue for "rapping" makes it so easy. So acceptable. So "in." Such a comfortable contributor to the collective conversational compost heap.

"They"

We all know our (acquired) tendency to seek a scapegoat to excuse our weaknesses, our apathy, our failure to realize our full potential. "They" can stand for parents, the university's board of trustees, all adults, the company, "the brass," organized labor, whoever the enemy is conceived to be. Undoubtedly the equivalent is used among Russian and Chinese Communists to refer to one another—or to the free world.

Sometimes "they" are held up as bogeymen who lie in wait to punish disobedience or nonconformity. Thus mother says to daughter: "What will 'they' think of you, with your hair all uncombed like that? You'll never get admitted to any *decent* college." And the new employee is told by an old-timer: "Better not make that suggestion about the work. 'They' don't like too much initiative around here."

There is always, of course, the definite implication that the speaker is dissociating himself from what he says. The culprit is that shadowy "thing," a handy means of sloughing off responsibility or avoiding a decision that should rightly be one's own. Take the supervisor of the typing pool who has just had to tell one of her workers that there is to be no increase in pay. "They won't let me give you anything." The idea planted in the typist's mind is that "someone in Personnel" dislikes her; the raise is being withheld in spite of company policy—whereas the fact is that the girl's performance does not rate an increase. The supervisor just *doesn't have the nerve* to say so.

Managers at all levels of an organization are prone to use the next-higher level as a scapegoat in this fashion. When they speak of their superiors as "they," they may be quite consciously refusing to accept responsibility for the decision or order they are communicating; they are pretending not to be part of management. Basically, however, they are hating themselves and, therefore, hating and distrusting their fellow managers.

Dialogue

You certainly know about those speakers who visit the campuses as representatives of the "straight" world and say, "Let's rap! Let's have a dialogue!" Maybe, if you're young enough, you've listened to them yourself. "You're the greatest generation in our history," say these speakers.

To them we say here, "How naive and patronizing can you be?" Far better to tell such an audience: "I don't *know* how good—or how bad—you are. And *you* don't, either. Only results will tell. Let's sweep the pink clouds out of the way and target some specific five- and ten-year objectives. We'll know how bright and how able—how relevant—you are *then*."

A Pattern for Change

There ought to be

1. Task forces specifically charged with the mission or objective of researching *change in all its dimensions.* The new feature of this probing would be its focus on *potentials* for change: economic, social, political, and spiritual. We would then begin to see a massive shift in the use of foundation-fund allocations from what has impeded—or will impede—progress in human actualization (studies, for instance, of *courage* rather than *fear*) to what will free, stimulate, and expand man's total effectiveness, of which corporate or organizational effectiveness is an integral part.

2. Research into the root causes of paradoxical behavior and possible solutions of this problem. Listen to James Reston in a June 6, 1971, *New York Times* column entitled "To the Class of '71 . . . ." Of these university students just graduating he says:

> . . . Their situation is full of paradox. No generation ever talked so much about "commitment" yet seemed so unwilling to commit itself to one man or woman, or to one useful job of work. None has talked so much about the great political and social issues of the age, or written so badly about them. Seldom has so much physical and intellectual energy been combined, often in the same persons, with so much physical and intellectual slackness and even laziness. They talk about "participating democracy," but most of them don't participate in the democratic process. They complain about the loss of "individualism" but run in packs. They condemn the welfare state but lean on it and praise the good-life personal happiness but for all their activity often seem bored and singularly joyless.[1]

3. In this same connection, careful studies of the efficacy of

    a. Establishing a youth corps (but we need a better name for it). This would be composed of young people just out of secondary school—or at least in that age group—who would be assigned work in all sorts of carefully targeted areas of human need throughout our society.

    b. Requiring that a young person complete one or two years of such *hard work* before being admitted to college.

REFERENCE

1. James Reston, "To the Class of '71 . . . ," *The New York Times,* June 6, 1971.

12

Thy Neighbor
as Thyself

Iт should be perfectly clear to the reader who has come this far that he can learn to respect and admire others only as he becomes aware of his own potential. He can perceive, relate to, and help unleash the strength of others only if he knows his own. This may be the quintessence of the effective MANager's concern in the coming months and years.

Here we come to grips with the keystone, the quintessential block in the foundation of this book:

- Can we respect others if we do not respect ourselves?
- Can we identify others' strengths if we don't know ours?
- Can we help build the other person if we don't know our own building materials?
- Can we love and admire the other person if we do not have a proper sense of our personal worth?

Surely no rational person will question the need for a vast improvement in our capacity to combine and blend our various efforts to create a better world, a better society, a better community, a better company, department, section —or home. *Surely individual lives are enriched when we can interact with each other on a basis of perceived and respected strengths.*

The Toughest Assessment

"You want to know what's wrong with this company?" The listener said no, but the speaker went ahead anyway. "My staff has got no damned enthusiasm. I've been to the seminars, I've read the books on leadership and motivation. If I could just get some support, some enthusiasm from my people, we would really get things done."

The man who said this was pale and grim. He had a sullen, even petulant, expression and his eyes appeared almost extinguished.

What was this man really conveying? Asked to describe the strengths of some of his staff, the man raised his eyebrows abruptly. Almost in disbelief he echoed, "Strengths? What the hell do you want to talk about strengths for? We've got to figure out the weaknesses of these people if we're to get anywhere."

The other man had trouble concealing his impatience. He said, "I don't have the time to waste talking with you about vacuums; talking about zeros, about nothings. You see, the proper definition of a 'weakness' is 'the absence of a strength,' and there's precious little point to a lot of fuss about anything that's absent. Let's get at your people's strengths so that we know what kind of building material we have to work with."

The response: "Hell, I don't even know my own."

Yet isn't this really what it's all about? We have to look into that honest thing called a mirror and see peering back at us a man or a woman who knows something of his strengths, who has a healthy, mature, viable awareness of his abilities, who has been able to cultivate and maintain a measure of real self-esteem and is intent on improving it. Until we have done this, it is the only mature thing, it is the only practical and tough-minded thing, to recognize that we will not be able to see strengths in other people, particularly if they are of a different generation, color, race, creed, caste, class—you name it. We simply will not be able to identify and above all relate to—and help build on—others' strengths if there is not an adequate level of strength awareness confronting us in that mirror.

This, you see, is the toughest assessment of all. It becomes absolutely vital to be able to stare directly at our own strengths and recognize that if we perceive them, both present and potential, in full perspective, we usually will have very little recourse except further quest, further change, further growth, further effectiveness, further *use* of strength-nourished skills.

"Down the Labyrinthian Ways"

Consider carefully these familiar lines from *The Hound of Heaven*, by Francis Thompson:

I fled him down the nights and down the days,
I fled him down the arches of the years,

I fled him down the labyrinthian ways of my own mind,
And in the mist of tears, I hid from him,
And under running laughter up vistaed hopes I sped
And shot precipitated adown titanic glooms of chasmed fears.

Is our society in flight? Many voices of doom are telling us that we are fleeing from—who knows what? However, *if* such a flight is going on, it may be a flight from our own potential, from our own strengths. Perhaps—although it is better said, with semitheological overtones, in the lines of Francis Thompson—we are fleeing from an awareness of our ultimate selves.

Years of contemporary research, using the latest psychological, psychometric, and sociometric tools coupled with a searching analysis of the writings of the great thinkers of history, suggest strongly that we seldom fear the different or unfamiliar if we have sufficient awareness, understanding, and appreciation of that person whom we conceive ourselves to be. At all levels and at all ages, we ought to reverse the flight (if, indeed, we are engaged in one) from awareness or confrontation of our strengths and begin to cultivate that toughest of all emotions, that most difficult of all confrontations—adequate love of self.

The toughness which "loving our enemy" demands is obvious. It is patently impossible until we understand the "first and greatest" commandment, which ends: ". . . and thy neighbor as thyself."

Love—Is It Too Big for You?

Picture a group of Earth men landing their craft on a celestial body somewhere in Outer Space. Disembarking heavily armed and ready to defend themselves, they encounter living beings and—with weapons trained—begin a "dialogue." They soon discover that these representatives of an advanced form of life can speak any language the Earth men choose. However, it seems that the language on this distant planet is curiously devoid of invective and defense.

"You Earth men," says the spokesman for the welcoming committee, "use two words we have never heard of—*hate* and *fear*. They just haven't been invented here. And, incidentally, why do you people carry weapons? Is there something here that we don't understand? Can you explain it?"

Well? *Can* we? What would happen to the "prob._m " between the generations if hate and fear could be supplanted by those tough and daunting words *love* and *courage?* What are the implications for our jobs? Our homes? Our lives?

He's Different; Ergo, We Must Fear Him

The alleged communication gap between the young M.B.A. and his semi-obsolete boss has become virtually a cliché. It is safe to assume, however, that the faults and weaknesses, like the resulting problems, are about evenly divided. Both sides can generally learn a good bit from the other.

This is why it has become so important—even crucial— that we sharply accelerate the rate at which we are learning to understand ourselves. Well enough, that is, to better understand each other. We badly need to develop new training methods and materials in this area.

127

Do you suppose this is what the Great Commandment intended in the dictum "Love thy neighbor as thyself"?

A Pattern for Change

Why not undertake

1. Research to determine the individual and group motives which have seemingly fostered a rejection of the great philosophers of the past (or, at least, many masters of today's communications media would have us believe that Socrates, Aristotle, Kant, William James, and other tough-minded thinkers have been rejected). It may well be that the intellectual and spiritual rigors of *applying* ancient truths have daunted many people who have not possessed sufficient self-respect and self-love. Let us apply the best of our modern research instruments to the validation—or nullification—of this premise.
2. Research to determine the elements of commonality between the great leaders of history and the greatest contemporary leaders. Such research should not be restricted in time or place. The principal criterion in selecting the researchers should be demonstrated ability to achieve a high level of sound, honorable results. Here again, as a criterion of "honorable," we submit that researchers must penetrate beyond doubt and learn to *doubt their doubts*.

Perrin Stryker has said that the twentieth century may be "recorded as the epoch in which men for the first time attempted to cultivate methodically, and on a large scale, a class of superior managers." This means leaders in all areas of human endeavor. It has not happened yet, but we can and must make a beginning soon! Research that yields a clear, meaningful profile of *greatness* can provide real guidance in taking the first step.

13

Isn't It Strange . . . ?

We have made a great deal, in these pages, of the importance of hard work. And of obstacles to overcome. The evidence for this point of view is all around us. It's a funny thing, but those people who appear to have it made from childhood—so to speak—by birth, rank, and perquisites often do not make it in the end, whereas the good old American hard work succeeds dramatically for other people with few advantages to start.

So what about the tested American verities? Are they subdued, substandard, or only subliminal? What's been happening to young people who haven't encountered some real gut-level difficulties?

Two Behaviors, Two Intents

Before attempting to answer this question, let's take an unabashed and—yes—unapologetic look at a device alluded to previously in this book. It is often used in group dynamics or what are sometimes called encounter sessions. Each person present is asked to point a finger at someone else in the group—and keep it pointed. People sit there feeling puzzled, amused, resentful, or foolish as the case may be. Then the leader suggests that each take a long look at the three fingers pointing back at himself.

This little trick serves to illustrate that two patterns of behavior often accompany two patterns of intent. If we really want to build up a person, group, or thing, we must keep the onus of actuation, leadership, and/or example *on us*. In short, we must shape ourselves up before attempting to shape up others. But, if we don't really want to commit ourselves to change and growth, we can expediently opt for the other alternative and say in effect: "If *you'll* just get on the ball, then I, your parent, boss, or leader, can demonstrate how much *I* am on the ball. . . ."

Life as a Series of Options

> Isn't it strange that princes and kings,
> And clowns that caper in sawdust rings,
> And common people like you and me.
> Are builders for eternity,
> Each is given a bag of tools,
> A shapeless mass, a book of rules,
> And each must make ere life has flown,
> A stumbling block or a stepping stone.[1]

One of the beautiful (and we use the word thoughtfully and confidently) things about our free enterprise system, which provides for freedom of economic, social, political, and spiritual enterprise, is that it offers us one of the most precious gifts human beings can have—that is, the opportunity to choose.

Life, we are saying here, is a series of options. For instance, if we believe with Dr. Charles F. Kettering, the late executive and inventor at General Motors, that "we had better be concerned about the future because we're going to spend the rest of our lives there," we must continually be choosing from a variety of options. If we believe, further, that no one can live perpetually in neutral and that, accordingly, we substantially build or destroy every day in reacting to people, policies, procedures, processes, and practices, then isn't it only good sense to do some tough thinking about options?

Man's Needs for Self-actualization*		Opposites
Truth	LIFE	Lies
Goodness		Evil
Aliveness		Deadness
Individuality		Conformity
Perfection		Ugliness
Necessity		Expediency
Completion		Abandonment
Justice		Inequity
Order		Chaos
Simplicity	CHOOSE	Complexity
Richness		Poverty
Playfulness		Grimness
Effortlessness		Tightness
Self-sufficiency		Dependency
Meaningfulness		Meaninglessness
Self-esteem		Self-denigration
Esteem by others	DEATH	Contempt by others
Love and belongingness		Hate and alienation

*According to Maslow's hierarchy as reported in Frank Goble, The Third Force (New York: Grossman Publishers), 1970, p. 50. Reprinted by permission.

132

Stern, disciplined reflection about values is the essential underpinning for all relevant change in the relationships both between generations and between peers—on the job and off the job. The accompanying diagram shows a set of alternatives. Do you dare to choose clearly without hedging?

The Synergistic Gyroscope

Dr. Daniel Yankelovich said back in 1966, "On the whole, . . . today's youth shares the same beliefs and values as older people. It may be slightly more optimistic or ebullient in spirit, but overall it reflects the mood and direction of the rest of the nation." [2]

This is surely true today; however, the *external manifestations* of the internal gyroscopes (or value systems) of today's youth would seem to have changed. Young people have, in fact, become more and more cynical as they look for *evidence of the efficacy* of the older generation's values.

The existing evidence is considerable but is all too often obscured by our previously discussed dialogue of doom. We often see a sharp dichotomy in young people on campuses. One group is pursuing values that build values; we could liken them to David Riesman's "other-directed" group. The other seems committed to the reverse. The first is synergistic, moving and growing outward (explosively?). The second is fragmentative, becoming a receiving set for tensions and fears (implosively?). Investigation often establishes a direct link between a young person's values and the "dialogue" used in the family during the formative years.

Values that build values; strengths that build strengths.

That is what is wanted, because new strengths cannot possibly derive from weaknesses. Weaknesses are the absence of strengths or, in other words, a vacuum. New strengths—or insights or values—can come only through the discovery of potential strengths, dormant yet implicit in use, and through the further development of present strengths.

"Life's Inmost Secret"

"If anything is that easy, is it really worth that much?" This is the watchword of those men and women who have opted for true values. It is an actualization; it *sounds* energetic, and so are the people it describes. It is the end result of finding that one's dreams, desires, and disappointments are stepping-stones toward greater goals and communication with other individuals.

Dreams, desires, and disappointments. What are these, essentially? Dreams are challenges, nourished by visions and evanescent wishes, that keep a mind questing. Desires are what keep the dreams alive. And disappointments are mind-toughening experiments which enable the dreams to continue even though realization may seem beyond the horizon.

Perhaps, in recent years, no writer has been more widely read on campuses throughout the nation than Kahlil Gibran, the Lebanese poet, philosopher, theologian, and man for all seasons. Listen to what he is saying:

> Always you have been told that work is a curse, and labor is a misfortune. But I say to you that when you work you fulfill a part of earth's furthest dream, assigned to you when that dream was born. And in keeping yourself in labor you

are in truth loving life. And, to love life through labor is to
be intimate with life's inmost secret.[3]

Many mature people read this particular quotation and
say: "Wouldn't it be great if my son [or daughter] really
believed in that kind of thing?" And at least an equal
number of young people have quoted the same words
and said: "Wouldn't it be great if my father [or mother]
could view life in the same wonderful way that Gibran
saw it?" It's high time that both young and old tested the
truth of Gibran's words for themselves, discovering the
relationship between dreams, desires, and disappointments
on the one hand and the realization of universal goals and
values on the other.

My Book of Rules

Can an organization have values as well as an individual? Absolutely! These are embodied in its philosophy of
management—its rule book.

"A management philosophy, eh? Management creeds,
statements of 'principle,' management's mission, big dreams
—what in the world do all these have to do with running
a profitable business? I want to talk profit and nuts and
bolts. That's the only rule book I understand."

In seminars and other developmental sessions of various
kinds the participants are often asked to state which they
consider to be the most successful, best managed, and
profitable company in the country—perhaps in the world.
The bulk of the responses usually name IBM. It would
therefore seem appropriate to listen to Thomas J. Watson,
Jr., IBM's chairman of the board, as he shares some insights
in *A Business and Its Beliefs*. The book is subtitled *The*

Ideas That Helped Build IBM, and in it Watson lays out three fundamental beliefs which he says form the core of a profitable company's philosophy:

> . . . Our respect for the individual.
>
> We want to give the best customer service of any company in the world.
>
> We believe that an organization should pursue all tasks with the idea that they can be accomplished in a superior fashion. IBM *expects* and *demands* [italics ours] superior performance from its people in whatever they do.

So simple and yet so tough. So brief and yet so powerful.

One of the major reasons for IBM's particularly great success is the fact that the fundamental foundation of the organization cuts right to the heart of the human condition —to the need for *significance,* the need for identification with something bigger than self, the need to respect oneself before one can respect others. By great *service,* we build not only abundance of the pocketbook but abundance and actualization of the spirit. Profitable? Decide for yourself!

Finally, two more quotations from Watson:

> This, then, is my thesis: I firmly believe that any organization, in order to survive and achieve success, must have a sound set of beliefs on which it premises all its policies and actions.
> . . .
> If you hire good people and treat them well, they will try to do a good job. They will stimulate one another by their vigor and example.[4]

Have you checked *your* rule book lately?

A Pattern for Change

To see the individual in perspective it is vital to better understand the society of which he is a part. Of course, this cuts both ways—it is a fact that a society is the product of its individuals. Leadership insight, managerial awareness—these are acutely necessary as we *mentally* tool for a future that can but needn't be bewildering. (Herman Kahn, in fact, predicts that the 1990s will be "glorious.")

Max Ways, in his keen and insightful *Fortune* series entitled "The U.S. Economy in an Age of Uncertainty," says:

> . . . All the expensive U.S. hardware, bought after shrewd and complex cost-benefit calculations, could not overcome certain non-quantifiable reactions in the "minds of men."

And:

> In nearly all the domestic government functions that will be important in the Seventies, actual decision making will be very widely dispensed among millions of *minds* and *wills* [italics ours] that cannot be coerced or bought.

And the last paragraph of all in the book-length series:

> If in the Seventies the U.S. comes to understand the nature of its new governmental problems, if it begins to make visible headway in dealing with the challenge of expanding prosperity and freedom, then the present demoralization will be dispelled. Nothing would be better for the economy than a restored *confidence* [italics ours] that government can handle the political needs of the "new nation." [5]

A new nation it can certainly be! But do you see what we must do? It is imperative that our entire focus begin to shift from *externals* to *internals*. From the belief that management consists of "doing things with things" or even "getting things done through people" to a virtual crash program for understanding the qualities of mind and soul that in reality comprise the central motor of all constructive individual and group endeavor.

Needed: confidence, commitment, insight, work, and more confidence. Are these needed words a part of your daily conversation at home, at work, everywhere?

REFERENCES

1. R. L. Sharpe, "A Bag of Tools," in *The Best Loved Poems of the American People* (New York: Doubleday, 1936).
2. "Youth and the Establishment: A Report on Research for John D. Rockefeller 3rd and the Task Force on Youth by Daniel Yankelovich Inc.," February 1, 1971, p. 75.
3. Reprinted from *The Prophet,* by Kahlil Gibran, with permission of the publisher, Alfred A. Knopf, Inc. Copyright 1923 by Kahlil Gibran; renewal copyright 1951 by Administrators C.T.A. of Kahlil Gibran Estate, and Mary G. Gibran.
4. From *A Business and Its Beliefs* by Thomas J. Watson, Jr. Copyright 1963 by McGraw-Hill. Used with permission of McGraw-Hill Book Company.
5. Max Ways, "The U.S. Economy in an Age of Uncertainty," *Fortune* (August 1971).

14

Who's Tired?

Who needs lots of good hard work? We all do! But does this have to mean grim, taut faces, gray with fatigue, and terse, curt exchanges instead of real communication? Not in the least!

It is not uncommon to greet a junior executive, a senior executive, a student, a faculty member, a news vendor—in fact, anybody in virtually any walk of life— during the day and be rewarded with a pallid-to-grumpy bit of conversation like this: "How are you this morning?" "Oh, not too bad." Or: "Good morning." "What's good about it?" Or: "Hey, have you heard about . . . ?" "Who cares?" Or: "How do you feel?" "Rotten." Yet how often do you hear active people—really busy people—engaged in uttering these banalities? They are too busy achieving that goal bigger than self.

Who's Bored? The Fatigue Syndrome

Badly needed are carefully targeted research programs that would explore the causes of productive, actualizing behavior leading to real achievement—the behavior of people who accomplish much, not out of boredom or fatigue, but because they have a high level of energy, verve, and enthusiasm and they love constructive work.

A personal friend, who is a noted businessman and consultant, gives us the following examples of people who learned how *good* it can feel to be honestly tired:

> A young man who had done little physical work in his life encountered one of life's pleasures in his junior year in high school. He had been sheltered at home as an only child, never looked for work because he "wasn't seventeen yet," lay around during the summer and watched TV. His first job, working for a small-town parks department, required him to perspire, work hard, and get dirty. But his comment after a week's work was: "It's fun being refreshingly tired." And he has continued to work hard since he learned the rewards of physical exertion—he looks, feels, and *sounds* better.

And:

> It's amazing what practical experience can do to teach the principles and benefits of hard work and free enterprise. A small boy of 11 complained of the work involved in hoeing watermelons, but in one day had a different attitude. That change came about when he alone manned the watermelon sales stand and sold $42.00 worth of melons, of which he received a percentage. He had become a businessman, not just a laborer.

Now look back at the cocktail party and the slightly "high" ladies who all seem identical in their efforts to impress, to show clearly who has the most self-confidence, the most fun. When it seems imperative to rush up to people with ice cubes sloshing and say, "Gosh, isn't this *fun?*" a party becomes deadly dull. A know-it-all cynic—a man who knows the price of everything and the value of nothing—may become the center of attention because of his loud jokes, but he soon sees his crowd drifting away and ignoring him.

Who becomes bored? Everyone who must listen to constant negatives and expedients. Who are the bores? Whoever engages in these monologues of doom. Yes, monologues—because the general reaction to sarcasm and cynicism precludes any normal human exchange.

People are inclined to lose sight of all that touches the senses. So many students in particular are engrossed in studies and the usual varied campus activities to the point where they know nothing about what goes on out in the everyday *real* world. They are engulfed in a fatigue syndrome. And their regular reply to "How are you?" becomes "So *tired!*"

More About the Capacity for Wonder

We have already mentioned the importance of retaining through life the sense of wonder that we see in children. The child is unself-conscious; he responds unashamedly to the world around him. Yet his elders, too often, are afraid to show amazement, wonder, awe; they worry for fear people may think them unsophisticated, childish. It's so easy—too easy—to stay on the periphery of the world and let the beauty and fascination of life slide by.

What an antidote to boredom wonder can be, though! At any age!

At a North Carolina university, a gifted astronomy professor named Philip S. Riggs watched a total solar eclipse for the first time and was inspired to poetry:

Fifteen hundred miles behind me, and again ahead
I stand in awed anticipation.
A lifetime I have waited for these moments.

Three sublime minutes,
not to be repeated here for centuries,
are about to begin.

Under the hair-thin crescent sun,
Weird, orangish midday twilight
fades fast over the serene fields and woods.

A rush of darkening gray sweeps in.
From around the horizon faint, roseate light
suffuses the stilled landscape and the darkened air above.

High above a hushed and quiet earth,
white-hot brilliance, fading quickly outward,
rings the hard, black moon-disk
Beyond, like far-away, luminous spun-glass wisps
softly lighted against the slate-dark sky,
extending long, wide, tapering jets of sheerest,
fragile gray-white,
streams out a million miles
the evanescent Corona . . .
diaphanous, gossamer;
ineffable loveliness.

My mind and spirit,
freed by quiet solitude, enchanted,
drink in with throat-tightening emotion
the wondrous, delicate beauty.

. . .

Suddenly, behind me, the swish of an automobile!
Oh Man!—pathetic Man!
What *are* you?
Where has gone the vision of your mind,
where the wings of your spirit? [1]

This dedicated man has studied and lived astronomy all his life, yet he still can feel awed by nature and rhapsodize over it. Compare him for a moment to a group of students who listened to his poem at a Midwestern university. During a class session on the solar eclipse, they slept routinely through the professor's lecture. When he talked about the excitement he himself felt as he witnessed this natural phenomenon, snickers and contrived laughter broke out. After class there were sarcastic remarks and nasty put-downs.

These young people were terribly bored with the whole idea of being as excited as their teacher professed to be. Who cares? was their attitude. Why bother? Why indeed— except that with years and years of life's high moments yet to experience, it seems *such a waste* for them to start closing their senses to the vibrations of nature. And this is exactly what they are doing when they spend hours engaging in "dialogue" in student unions and dormitories, saturating their minds with the ideas of their peer groups elsewhere and the teachings of the latest folk "hero." To deliberately shut out the rich repository of wonder available from people like this gifted professor is not only sad, it is potentially dangerous and tragic.

The major complaint of many students about the Establishment is that its representatives don't feel or live or know the value of life. Are they themselves any better, one may ask, with their everlasting talk, talk, talk? What right have such kids, then, to ridicule an older man who can still feel excitement and awe? Possibly because to believe in that emotional response would be to obviate the hypocrisy of so-called "thinkers" who sneer and complain about adults not caring.

Tom Runciman, a young man who *does* live life beyond the fringes of involvement, wrote simply and pungently:

> They called us names—
>   You and I
> They called us weird and crazy.
> But most of all they called us
>   Foolish kids.
> Yet, they sat inside and talked their
>   grown-up gossips,
> While two foolish kids sat on
>   nature's porch
> And enjoyed one stormy night.[2]

Here we have evidence of two very similar and beautiful life philosophies, of an enjoyment of nature far above many men's petty thoughts and gripes. More importantly, we are rising above the distinction of generations. Quite a gap might be expected between the ages of 20 and 75. But, if we read the poems carefully, we see there is none!

Growing older does have, and should have, a beauty of its own, if the spirit remains vibrant and the mind resilient and tough. The unlined, characterless features of youth may have a wondering and innocent attractiveness of their own, but no less does the weathered face of age, when it has learned from experience and not merely become a captive of it.

One Mind to Another

So why are too many adults caught up in the thought that they can't communicate with their college-age children and vice versa? Probably because that same old word "dialogue" keeps popping up. The mouths open and emit words, but no telegraph lines link one mind with another. Why? Because communication between the generations has been deteriorating for years. Instead of communication (which we define as shared meaning, shared understanding), we have a mass of published material saying, "Oh, yes, there's a generation gap, it's inevitable, but these young people are the best generation we have had come along in quite a while." Or: "This generation is one of the most rotten in history."

Bah! First of all, the stereotyped youth/parent "gap" is nonexistent unless members of one generation begin to close their minds before pretending to listen. Second, no particular child/father or child/mother combination can afford to succumb to the image of relationships between the generations built by someone else. Each child in each family must have his or her own individual type of relationship with his parents, and no amount of research or "child psychology" is going to help close a gap unless each child is regarded as a person with individual emotions and a capacity for love.

There are, of course, many difficulties—perhaps embarrassments—to be faced when two people bare their souls, so to speak, and try to communicate. But isn't it worth a try? Wouldn't you like to show somebody else that you really do care what happens to his life? Wouldn't you rejoice if you could feel that your parents or children felt (deep inside, maybe) an intense interest in your success as a happy, fulfilled person?

This holds good, too, for communication between a young person and any adult. It might be difficult at first, say, for our two poetry writers—though only until they bridged the confidence chasm. This has opened mostly because of a mystique that's been bandied about far too much lately: A gap in age seemingly must cause a gap in ideas. One group is "young and idealistic," while the other has come to be "sedentary and materialistic." Not necessarily. Two individuals caught up by even a small example of nature's magic should be able to absorb each other's ideas easily; it shouldn't require a solar eclipse.

Unfortunately, worry about the generation gap and the confidence chasm creates difficulties because neither side is sure enough of himself to let down his guard and listen to the other objectively, without prejudice. It's the old problem: People are afraid of appearing foolish if they share the thoughts they cherish privately.

Quality and the Quality Seekers

One area of disagreement that is commonly held to be aggravating the confidence chasm has to do with *quality*. Young people are said to feel—and rightly, the implication is—that their elders, if they ever cared for quality, have long since settled for shoddiness: in their personal lives and in the products and services which they are responsible for providing to others.

True, there has been a rash of quality seekers lately. The success of Ralph Nader's efforts is certainly proof of this. So is the fact that among young people the biggest single objection to going into business is the apparent lack, in too many organizations, of a real concern for quality. A

146

poll taken during discussions with 30 college seniors major-
ing in management gave the following results: 18 wanted
to go into small entrepreneurial-type businesses even if
their salary was lower than what they might earn as junior
executives in larger companies; 10 wanted to start their
own businesses; and 2 preferred junior executive jobs.

Why did so many want their own businesses? It may
have been because they didn't want to end up having to
follow the policies of numerous companies which stress
quantity production. What is troubling most of the companies that stress quantity—in contrast to the corporate
quality seekers (there *are* a few, which may come as news
to some young critics)—is overhead. More important,
though, they are suffering from the current shortage of
qualified, and quality-conscious, minds. The newly turned-
out graduates avoid them; thus a vicious circle forms.

Perhaps in all generations the truly quality-conscious
individual has been in fairly short supply. What is new,
possibly, is the idea that an organization can and should be
quality-conscious—indeed, has an obligation to the community to produce quality products and services. And it
can do just that. As in personal living, the secret is to begin
with a basic goal and set of values, calmly and systematically intertwining positive ideals with practicality. The
end result is an organization painstakingly constructed
and soundly entrenched in success, with a fine kind of self-
satisfaction as an intrinsic reward.

Never Stop Reaching

But a caution to the *relatively* quality-conscious and
successful: After reaching your "final" goal, remember to

set another one higher up. The threat to so many, once they have arrived at a particular point, becomes the secure thought of "I've made it. Now I can relax—take it easy." And, as body and mind begin to rest, then solidify and become inactive, so do the wellsprings of satisfaction and achievement.

Even though the next goal set must be one quite unrelated to your usual business, school, or family concerns, set it. Stretch your mind—otherwise you will risk decay of mental muscles. A muscle that is not used will deteriorate. A life that is unused will slip by and vanish as though it had never been.

So, today, try to reach a little further than you felt was possible yesterday. Find new muscle tone and the ability to get up again as life continues to do things to (or for) you.

More Than Just Lip Service

Recently, a 27-year-old M.B.A. who looked even younger was assigned to study a major department in the company in which he was employed. His crisp, organized report called for changes that would cut paperwork and related facilities by some 36 percent. His findings and recommendations were supported by comprehensive charts and data.

The department head attacked the report as "useless, idiotic, immature." Shortly thereafter, the young man accepted a position with a management consulting firm and moved to another part of the country. Thus he provided no further competition for the older man. Moreover, he allowed the department head to present the controversial report, after careful review and major modification, as having been prepared by him. Subsequently, every recommended change was carried out and red tape was vastly reduced.

A perhaps not too surprising residual result was that the department head seemed younger and more vital. He was now engaged in work that was significantly altering the shape, style, and direction of his organization. The gifted young M.B.A. had painstakingly tied all the proposed changes to productive objectives. And, now that the threat of competition was removed, the mature executive, who had not had the benefit of the young man's careful educational tooling, began to do more than just give lip service to management by objectives. He actually began to enjoy the process.

The older man's doctor, who had considered him to have a dangerous coronary profile, now reported that the executive's health and spirits had improved significantly. This story may sound a little contrived, but it should provide real insight into what happens when you escape from the fatigue syndrome, discover a new zest and eagerness for living, and apply this newfound enthusiasm to the search for quality.

A Pattern for Change

Research should be imaginatively launched which will go far beyond the traditional studies of fatigue undertaken by industrial psychologists. These have yielded few catalysts for change. The new research should be targeted squarely on the *achiever*—at all ages—so that we can build on the accumulated findings. For instance, what produces vigor? It will be crucial, of course, to study such achievers in a 24-hour-a-day context—that of the "whole man."

In this context, ponder the words of one of the great pioneers in American psychology, William James:

> I have no doubt whatever that most people live, whether physically, intellectually or morally, in a very restricted circle of their potential being. . . . The so-called "normal man" of commerce, so to speak, the healthy Philistine, is a mere extract from the potentially realized individual he represents, and we all have reservoirs of life to draw upon of which we do not dream.[3]

James believed that the average person was only using about 10 percent of his potential. This is supported by an increasing amount of modern research. We therefore propose a sharply accelerated rate of expenditure, research, and experimentation toward the end of achieving whole-man status for every human being.

REFERENCES

1. Philip S. Riggs, untitled, unpublished poem. Copyright 1972 by Philip S. Riggs.
2. Tom Runciman, "One Stormy Night," unpublished poem. Copyright 1972 by Tom Runciman.
3. William James, *The Letters of William James* (Boston: Atlantic–Little, Brown, 1920).

15

Blessed Are the Debonair

WHAT has caused so many people of all ages to lose the sense of wonder which we saw in our previous chapter was so crucial in retaining a zest for life? What has happened to their capacity for dreaming, for seeing visions? We might say that they have become prisoners of their own tensions and frustrations and their self-imposed isolation from other people. They can never relax long enough to respond naturally to what is beautiful and worthwhile in the world in which they live or to signals from their fellow human beings.

The ability to relax is the key here. Only if we will let ourselves be "loose" can we be open to others' ideas, ideals, good intentions, and efforts to communicate. Only in this way can we be aware of our true identity.

We hear a great deal about "encounter sessions" and the benefits that lonely, tensed-up, disturbed men and women are deriving even, in some cases, from the mere touch of another person. But what more is an "encounter," really, than the result of opening up all our senses to the knowledge of others and, in the process, getting to know ourselves too?

Each in the Shell of His Frustrations

About two years ago, a visitor to San Francisco was walking in Golden Gate Park near the Haight-Ashbury section. Enjoying the sunlit afternoon, he paused to sit for a while on a bench. Presently he saw three people walking toward him. From a distance it was difficult to tell whether they were male or female. His attention wandered, but a moment later he felt a hand on his shoulder.

"Pardon me, sir. Are you a policeman?" asked a girl's voice.

"No," said the stranger, "I'm not."

"Well, go to hell, then," retorted the girl, and she walked off with a flip of her backside as the two young men with her giggled.

The man on the bench called out, "Hold on a minute—I'm not a policeman. There are three of you. We're right out here in the open, so come back and sit down. Let's talk a little bit."

The three obeyed, but before very long the two young men got up and stalked away. The visitor then began to talk to the young woman, who turned out to be 19 years old. She had come to San Francisco from a city in the Midwest—a sizable metropolitan center—where her father held a reasonably good executive position in a respected company. He was looked upon as a solid fellow in the community and was in his early forties. Now his daughter was living the strange life of Haight-Ashbury.

How It Starts

The girl was obviously unhealthy. Her lower lip was split, and from time to time she would dab with a soiled Kleenex at the blood that ran down her chin. But her voice was resonant, she had an excellent vocabulary, and she gave every indication of superior mental gifts. The man chatted with her for quite a while, and the two established a rapport.

Finally, the man risked a probing question: "When did all this begin—this business of living out here in the hippie commune and so on?"

"Well," the girl said, "I guess it all started when I was a sophomore in high school. One day I wanted to talk with Dad about some of my confusions and some problems that had come up the night before on a date. I hadn't been dating very long, and felt that if I had any serious questions, the obvious, logical person to talk to—from what I'd heard—was Dad. And so I recall asking hesitantly if he would talk to me about dating.

"At once Dad put his paper down and demanded, 'Why? What's happened?' I explained rather timidly that *nothing* had happened, but I wanted some information. I then asked some questions—none of them, as I remember, very bad and certainly not shocking at all—but Dad looked stunned.

"Pretty soon he was asking, 'What are you, some kind of tramp?'

"I felt a rush of humiliation and began to cry. It seemed as though nobody must really trust me if my own father took my questions—which until then, I assure you, were innocent—as signs of depravity and *assumed the worst.*

After that," said the girl, "we no longer had any communication, we had dialogue."

No Trust, No Love, No Joy

There it was, the distinction between those two words. The girl pointed out over and over how dialogue can take place with pitifully little real communication—much less a trusting, sensitive, meaningful relationship.

This girl had gone on through high school with fine grades and then entered college—where, during the first part of her first year, she was an honor student. She came home about Easter time, she said, and she doesn't quite know how this came about, but suddenly it hit her. At Easter the family was always in the mood to go to church and ostensibly to feel the Easter spirit. All at once, however, it struck her with a devastating force that she didn't want to be like her parents.

Why?

"Oh," said the girl, "they never seemed to have any fun. They were sour. They were grim and competitive even about the business of going to church that Easter morning. They fussed about how they would look and whom they would see, and the whole performance had no trace of joy, no gladness, no lifting of spirit."

What, as she looked back, would she have liked her father to do or say on that particular day when she was 16 and asked him her questions about dating?

She replied slowly: "I never insisted on believing that my father was any kind of oracle or genius, but I wish he had just walked across the room to me that day as I began to cry, put his hand on my shoulder and his arm around me, and said 'You're my little girl, and I love you. I don't really know all the answers, but if we keep talking enough, and sharing enough, I'm sure that we can work things out.' That's all I ever really wanted of him."

The Decision: Opting Out

It wasn't till a while after Easter, though, that the full realization hit her—in an almost terrifyingly urgent way— that she literally couldn't bear to follow in her mother's and father's footsteps. The following week she took off for Haight-Ashbury.

"What happened after you got here?" asked the man on the bench innocently. "Did you start smoking a lot of pot?"

Her voice became shrill. "What do you care about that?"

"I'd just like to know."

"Of course I smoke pot," she said.

"Do you think it's addictive?" asked the man.

"Oh, not chemically, of course, but I wonder when squares like you are going to start realizing that when kids smoke pot; when, at the same time, they feel down inside that they're not loved; when they don't like themselves and are convinced that there's nothing in life to look forward to, then they're going to go on to stronger stuff?"

"Are you on anything else right now?" asked the stranger.

"Why? Do you think I look like I am?" the girl demanded. Suddenly her eyes filled with tears, and her voice became hysterical in the fullest sense of the word. "Do you know what's going to happen to me, mister?"

"No," was the answer.

"I didn't think you did," retorted this young woman—and she pointed at the lesion in her lower lip. "I've got syphilis, can't you see? And I'm also on H" (which of course means heroin). "I'm going to die, you son-of-a-bitch, do you understand that? I'm going to die!" Then she got up and ran away out of sight, leaving the man in whom she'd confided to wonder just what eventually happened to another man's daughter.

Today's Acute Hunger

This anecdote reaffirms statements made, comments heard on many campuses and in many times and places. That is, it bears witness to the singular awareness, the acute hunger on the part of young people for some evidence that their parents and other adults they meet are *having fun*. In short, that the older generation's value system lends itself to a little joy, an occasional lift of the spirit. In the absence of this joy, young men and women all too often may simply conclude that the adult world is not for them.

Who, after all, wants deliberately to shape his or her life so as to emulate someone who usually seems to be tired, tense, distrustful, and unhappy?

What Makes the Difference?

A few months after the experience in Golden Gate Park, however, a conversation took place between this same man and another 19-year-old girl. She had just described herself as "the happiest person in the world." Full of drive, enthusiasm, and sparkle, she told of her deep involvement in the community, the church, the campus; she radiated a force which seemed to say, "Life is good." She was by now operating her own small business—one offering a service—and could give a lucid description of the worth and requirements of the free enterprise system. And—oh, yes! Incidentally, though her features were perhaps not very pretty by conventional standards, she was unusually attractive.

The question was put to her: "What's the difference between you and most of the types who are over at the rock festival this weekend?" The answer was brief, tough, well thought out, and definite. "From the time I was a baby, my parents have given me abundant love and trust and have always expected me to do my best—within a framework of reason."

Let's underscore those words again right here: *love, trust, best, reason.* This girl by her own efforts had acquired the tensile strength to live with self-acceptance and self-trust, to stand with dignity and integrity, and to revel in her budding womanhood. But, you see, she had received the *right input.*

A Shift Toward the Positive

To be sure, if a young person from a hippie commune should read these lines, he might say, *"I've* never had the love and trust I'm told I need, so why should I change?" A flip answer in macrocosm might be, "Read the whole book." But here in microcosm is a serious reply.

"*You* seek happiness. What right have you, then, to

hate someone else and make life miserable for him? You say your parents failed to show their love and to trust you when you were a child. Maybe you think marriage and children aren't for you. If, however, you do raise a couple of children, do you want them to be as unhappy as you insist you are? If you don't, hadn't you better change— and *fast?* Forget about the reasons you have to *not* be happy. If your early life lacked the love of good parents and the companionship of understanding friends, don't dwell on your past. Instead of saying, 'I'm one of the unloved,' say, 'I *was* one of the unloved, but at last I've started to look for the warmth and affection and trust I've been missing.' "

Oh, sure, it's tough to change your whole way of thinking, but maybe a shift in a positive direction will clear away the cobwebs so you can see the love in others that you once were unable to believe in. The world has long since tired of hearing those old clichés about parents on the one hand ("They ruined my life!") and spoiled young good-for-nothings on the other. It's *about time* you and your elders alike decided to target in on some new goals.

Alternative to Alienation

The gloomy attitude that "nobody loves me" is undeniably selfish. When the "I'm not" syndrome takes over consciously or unconsciously, there is no recourse except to feel alienated. Perhaps a comment from Eric Hoffer will help us make our point more clear:

> There is a spoiled brat quality about the self-consciously alienated. Life must have a meaning, history must have a goal, and everything must be in apple-pie order if they are

to cease being alienated. Actually there is no alienation that a little power will not cure.[1]

Maybe the challenge of putting your life in order, not waiting for it to arrive there by itself, frightens you. If it does, try this: Instead of clinging to the security of passive criticism and inertia ("Let the other fellow fix it!"), lash out at yourself. Stop, look at the direction in which you are heading, and decide right now: "I will find love (trust, truth, strength to *do*) only if I search for it first in myself." Then start looking. You may be dumbfounded!

Old Values Are Not to Blame

It has often been said in recent years that at the root of many of the "hangups" existing among both the younger and the older groups in our society are the constrictive puritanism and traditional values which stem from the Protestant ethic or, more particularly, from the Judeo-Christian ethic on which many of our attitudes and assumptions are based. Reich, for instance, in *The Greening of America* seems to feel it has failed.

In this context it may be helpful to look at a newspaper column by Sydney Harris. It is entitled "Blessed Are the Debonair . . . ," and it goes like this:

Although the King James version of the Bible is one of the great literary triumphs of English, the translators did commit a few errors. One that has done grievous harm to Christianity over the centuries is the Beatitude "Blessed are the MEEK. . . ."

Meekness has become an unattractive word to us. We identify it with softness, with weakness, with passivity, with almost a propensity to enjoy insult, injury and self-martyrdom. To be "meek" is nearly to be cowardly in the modern lexicon. But this is not at all what the original wording meant, either in the Hebrew in the Old Testament or in the Greek of the New. The French Douay Bible comes much closer when it translates the Beatitude as: "Blessed are the DEBONAIR. . . ."

Strange as that sounds to Anglo-Saxon ears, "debonair," the dictionary tells us, is "of pleasant manners, courteous, gracious, charming, gay and carefree." In fact the twentieth-century idiomatic translation in America might faithfully read: "Blessed are the cool . . ." without committing a theological vulgarity. For "debonair" is much of what we mean when we describe a "cool cat." What we fail to understand is the moral and spiritual courage it takes to be "meek" in the fullest and deepest sense of the word. Far from being cowardly, it requires a heroism few of us are capable of. Jesus was asking his followers not to be grim and sour, or belligerent and argumentative as so many "religious" people of his time were. He knew that it was too easy to defend one's belief with name-calling and the brandishing of arms. The "meek or debonair" are far from weak, they possess an internal strength that permits them to suffer as St. Paul suffered without retaliation. When Jesus enjoined, "Pick up your cross, and follow me," he was not urging passivity but was calling for the supreme bravery of setting an example. This example of heroism and sacrifice for a belief was not to be performed in a smug and self-righteous manner, but in a gay and carefree manner "taking no heed for the morrow." The meekness in the gospel is a far cry from the bowed head, downcast eye of the slave; it is the quiet smile and the sure step of the only free man among us.[2]

Can any reader find even one statement in the Bible, Koran, Talmud, or any other great scriptural repository which suggests that the "good" person should be grim, blue-lipped, negative, or "puritanical"? We wonder, too, how many of us self-styled "moderns" possess the mental toughness to visualize traditional truths in a pragmatic, down-to-earth, seven-day-a-week way rather than lightly dismiss them as something for the "religious" to embrace on the Sabbath. Do we have the intellectual integrity to *doubt our doubts* and then apply our findings? Did the column by Mr. Harris sound "religious" to you? Some theologians define religion as "man's search for God" and Christianity as "God's search for man." We are not attempting religious comments of any kind but are seeking, rather, to help further reveal a tested and powerful—tough and beautiful—blueprint for LIVING.

The Message Misinterpreted

It should be a matter of great concern to us that the communication or confidence chasm has brought about a situation in which both generations seem to be yearning for greater gaiety, greater joy, but often in a wan, half-hearted manner. Their defense systems seem to rule gaiety and joy out of their vocabularies. Sad though it may be, strange though it may sound, they are in reality the victims—to some extent, at least—of an interpretation of the basic message of Christ which is quite unlike the interpretation which Sydney Harris has provided. Their sour outlook is precisely that of the 19-year-old Haight-Ashbury addict's parents as she described them.

The word so often communicated by the older generation to the younger is that life is a grim and dogged thing. One must proceed through it with one's guard up, figuratively and literally. The future belongs to the go-getter; there's something square and altogether vulnerable—perhaps even stupid—about the go-*giver*. Yet time after time, in seminars, encounter groups, "strength storming" sessions, and other kinds of experimental meetings across the country, it is clear that the yearning, the emptiness of a great many superficially "successful" people is a hunger for the mental and spiritual stuff possessed by those whom Mr. Harris has termed "the debonair."

. . . And the Love of Children

Does each generation realize that the other has this same deep hunger? *Does it?*

Said Ralph Waldo Emerson:

> To laugh often and much, to win the respect of intelligent people and affection of children; to earn the appreciation of honest critics and endure the betrayal of false friends; to appreciate beauty, to find the best in others; to leave the world a bit better, whether by a healthy child, a garden patch or a redeemed social condition; to know even one life has breathed easier because you have lived. This is to have succeeded.[3]

A Pattern for Change

Let us initiate research into the general and specific life-style components of the *free* manager, *free* employee, *free* citizen, *free* culture. The findings should be assessed and synthesized with a view to their best possible use in furthering a synergistic and viable society. Why? Both the costumes and the patois of our most determinedly nonconformist young people (and this should in no way be considered a mass indictment) so often suggest a dreadful and completely conformist lockstep. Yet their conversation usually is heavily suffused with an almost fervid concern about "freedom." Asked who wrote "Know the truth and the truth shall make you free," all too few are likely to know. In fact, nervous giggles and sidelong glances generally imply that anyone so foolish as to ask such a question must intend some kind of joke.

Since the earliest days of civilized man, one of the most important questions we have asked ourselves is, "What is truth?" Try hard to apply this question to every dimension of your life and your job. It can make your days more challenging, more growth-filled, and more *fun*.

REFERENCES

1. Eric Hoffer, *The Passionate State of Mind* (New York: Harper & Row, 1955).
2. Sydney J. Harris, "Blessed Are the Debonair," *Chicago Daily News,* February 19, 1971. Reprinted by permission of Sydney J. Harris and Publishers-Hall Syndicate.
3. As quoted in *Forbes* (December 1, 1971).

16

Meet the Actualizers

In summary, the message of these pages is just this: Think
of ME until ME is thoroughly thought through, and then
go on to show a wise ME by giving to others patience, love,
challenge, and compassion. In this way you can find yourself by losing yourself in service to man, your God, and
your country. You see, until we know who we are and
what we are, we simply can't *reach out and give* fully to
our fellow man. And until we have discussed, blended, and
blueprinted a satisfactory pattern of values, we cannot help
the generations—in their various forms of endeavor—to
perceive and concentrate on points of commonality or
consonance rather than give an undue emphasis to imagi-
nary or fragmented points of dissonance.

Cybernetics for All

The scientifically minded reader will, we hope, forgive
us if we speak in terms of *human* cybernetics. We concede

that our definitions go well beyond the ones found in most dictionaries.

To repeat, then, we have described a servomechanism as a flow of energy which returns to the source of its original impulse and—through the closed loop—renews its energy so that it is a form of perpetual motion, maintaining an ongoing, continuous force and resting on the physical truth that for every *action* there should, and can, be a *reaction*. We have said, too, that a cybernetic unit is a sophisticated version of a servomechanism possessing a built-in corrective guidance system.

Here in our last chapter, finally, we restate our premise that human beings are by far the most splendid cybernetic units of all and that, for optimum effectiveness, the fuel for these cybernetic units—*the value system of the individual mind*—must be stoked with cybernetic values. This is self-actualization indeed.

What Are Our Priorities?

In the glum world of *Future Shock* Alvin Toffler seems worried about "cyborgs," by which he means "human" units which will become fused with various cybernetic components in the purely metallic, plastic, or material sense. Perhaps it will happen—no one knows. However, the choice is ours; it can and must remain ours.

A committed search for further understanding of the great cybernetic truths and their application promises far greater physical, mental, and spiritual health and staying power than the application of the sort of purely electronic device that is so often described in a limited frame of ref erence as constituting "cybernetics." For instance, take the Biblical book called Proverbs. It is literally crammed with great truths which the times ache to see put into action; and the rich repository of such truths in the Sermon on the Mount needs no defense—only study, mastery, and *application*.

It's all a matter of what priorities we choose. And we can choose well if we do not apathetically abdicate those privileges and opportunities which are still greater today in the United States than in any other modern society in the world.

Lewis Mumford, the cultural historian, social philosopher, and urbanologist who is noted for his criticism of science, has said that our society's only hope lies in a return to human feelings and sensitivities, and to moral values, through "the increase of self-understanding, self-control, self-direction, and self-transcendence." In the same article, 46-year-old Dr. Edward E. Davis, Jr., science adviser to President Nixon, is quoted as saying he believes that "what we're seeing in the attack on science and technology is a power struggle between the 'two cultures,' the arts and sciences. I'm unhappy," he adds, "to see this kind of warfare. Basically, society needs a mix of science, humanities, and religion." [1] This is a warm and eclectic approach that can readily be endorsed.

Moreover, a warning: If these freedoms, these opportunities, these options—together with better "curricular fuel for choice"—are not taught throughout the fabric of our educational infrastructure, the predictions of Toffler can become a stark and terrifying reality.

Eric Hoffer describes the modern "cybernetically equipped" manager when he says:

The genuine creator creates something that has a life of its own, something that can exist and function without him. This is true not only of the writer, artist and scientist, but of creators in other fields. A creative organizer creates an organization that can function well without him. (How easy it is to give this simple lip service.) When a genuine leader has done his work his followers will say, "We have done it ourselves," and feel that they can do great things without a great leader. With the noncreative it is the other way around: In whatever they do, they arrange things so that they themselves become indispensable.[2]

We'll All Be Over Thirty

Richard L. Kattel is president of the Citizens and Southern National Bank of Atlanta, Georgia. What's unusual about that? True, he is only 35, but is this so remarkable? Not really. However, it may be instructive to hear some of his thoughts:

> Young men are just more willing to seek out innovative ways to earn bigger profits. Why? There is no rule that says if you risk capital and human resources you are not going to have a failure. Sure you learn from mistakes. But my father told me, and he was a banker, too, that the older you get the greater your fear of failing. That fear stops older executives from taking the risks that are necessary to build a company. But to the young executive, tomorrow is a new deal. So maybe he lost today. Tomorrow he'll double up and do a better job.

And in the same magazine article we read:

> "In five years or so," says Norton Simon's Dave Mahoney, "you will find the top men in business are going to be in their forties. They are not going to be the exception; they are going to be the rule."[3]

Clearly, one of the truly crucial problems of our time that *must* be faced is how to build a broad bridge of understanding between the giant organizations—many of them now unwieldy and floundering—so that they can more directly engage and utilize the vast number of potentially excellent young individuals who so badly need a feeling of commitment to meaningful goals which are larger than self.

The needs are here and now. The talents are here and now. But we must, for heaven's sake, drop our rigid old defenses and begin to connect and interconnect the two.

It's a great time to be alive! The cynic snickers at this declaration; he'd rather point out how awful things are. But reflect on it. Never in the recorded history of the world has a society been so acutely aware of its human needs. Never has a society contained such a rich and varied supply of physically and mentally healthy people—people whose material achievements now make it essential that they find actualization as *total* human complexes. Splendid complexes that must constantly cope with needs and solve problems to stay at the cutting edge of effectiveness, to push back continually the advancing frontier of innovative fulfillment.

Fine! If we're lucky, we'll all be over 30 some day—and isn't it great? We must view this hackneyed phrase, not as assurance that we're all bound to grow old and disillusioned and sink back together into mediocrity, but as a reminder that there will always be new and tougher thresholds to cross. And these thresholds, once crossed, will give us the opportunity to somehow fuse our aching need for personal achievement with the recognized needs of others—a fusion which lies at the heart of the good life.

Never Lose It!

A father was walking through the woods with Wendy, his nine-year-old daughter. They were holding hands, as fathers and daughters will.

Suddenly Wendy stopped and said, "Listen, Dad."

Dad listened, but couldn't hear a thing.

Then Wendy ordered, "Listen more closely, Dad. Do you hear that bird singing? Isn't it beautiful?"

At last Dad could hear it—and it was beautiful.

"Do you hear the wind in the trees?" Wendy asked next. "Isn't *it* beautiful?" And again Dad hadn't heard it before, but now he had and it, too, was beautiful.

As he stood there in the woods—he could still picture the scene clearly years later—the sun was streaming down on the face of this young child, whose face was completely devoid of cynicism or defense. She was vulnerable; she was letting in the wonder, the joy. The father reflected, as they walked on, that possibly this was what Christ meant when He said: "Except ye . . . become as little children, ye shall not enter into the kingdom of Heaven."

And now the scene changes to a hot, humid day in New York. Dad is walking through midtown Manhattan with a wise, thoughtful, discerning friend.

Suddenly the friend says, "Joe, I'm going to ask you the toughest question you have ever been asked." "Go ahead," says the other. "I've been asked some tough questions before."

"This will be your toughest," his friend insists. What is it? "If you could give one piece of advice to every child in the world as he or she turned 13, and you knew that advice was going to be taken seriously, what would it be?"

Dad thinks of quotations from the great philosophers.

Plato's saying: "Before you can move the world you must first move yourself." Aristotle's: "Lose yourself in productive work—in a way of excellence." Shakespeare's: "To thine own self be true" and "Sweet are the uses of adversity." He remembers Marcus Aurelius, who said, "Above all, *control* thyself"; Christ, who said, "Above all, *give* thyself"; Emerson, who said, "In the woods, we return to reason and faith." None of these, however, seems exactly right. They are perhaps too familiar, too glib.

And then the father's mind goes back to that day five years earlier when he walked through the woods with Wendy. "I know now what my one piece of advice would be," he says. " 'Never lose your sense of wonder. *Never* lose your sense of wonder.' "

The Prime Requirement

You may think there has been too much talk about wonder in this book. Yet it is the prime requirement of the tough mind; the open, questing, eager mind. It can provide the key to a wonder-full life. Perhaps, too, it may be one of the real secrets of retaining that quality which we have termed "debonair" for many years, so that life may be longer and richer and we may be able to relate much more meaningfully to the world around us.

But contrast this with Reich's vision in *The Greening of America*. He sees the child becoming "a skeptic of everything," innocence and wonder lost, adrift without the sure sense of parental love—unbelieving, cynical, betrayed.[4]

This dialogue of doom offers no stimulating, catalytic, constructive substance. It can only depress and stultify the real dreams, the eternal wonder, the questing spirit, the restless wonder-full innovative thrust so badly needed at all levels of our society. Organizations—whether business, government, educational, or religious—ought to be doing, and can in marvelous reality do, much to help provide the necessary guidance and thrust as we seek to realize our dreams for the future.

Beauty Is Truth

We are told, incidentally, that all the major breakthroughs in science throughout the ages have been the result of a passionate quest for truth and beauty by the scientist rather than a search for utility or application per se. Perhaps, then, there is practical ore to be mined by enriching our leadership and management development curricula to include much more emphasis on aesthetic perception and creativity.

Aristotle said, "Before you can do the noble, you must first do the useful." With this one can only agree. But the climb toward nobility of achievement—on a sound foundation of usefulness—possibly can be quickened when more and better programs among all strata of our society teach the dignity, beauty, and indeed the nobility of hard and demanding work, of tough and constructive achievement. It may be that nobility and usefulness are indivisible. It may be that the unabashed search for beauty at all levels of work and goal seeking can be the mortar.

Where did we get the "masculine mystique" that preoccupation with beautiful things is the sole province of the female? What is the basis of this stereotype? For stereotype it is! History is replete with evidence that both men and women of great achievement have been people who dreamed great dreams. And where do dreams spring from? From a passionate quest for beauty!

Our planet can become an ecological tragedy unless and until we reassess the true meaning and significance of beauty and nobility, neither of which can be separated from practical living. And people become what they say, remember? How long has it been since you gave your vocabulary a tough going-over for richness and beauty?

The Actualizer and the Actualized

"People without dreams. I don't know how they can live," said a 21-year-old coed. How indeed? But the dreams need not always be visible to the world at large.

Take the president of a certain manufacturing company. Tough-minded and pixielike—which would seem to be a paradox—he is a very real, a very successful, and an extremely happy man. In his sixties, this actualized individual—articulate, crisp, and fit—still takes off at a run to answer his telephone at the opposite end of his spacious stable, for he is a renowned horseman, admired for his equestrian accomplishments. The horse world, of course, knows relatively little about his personal or his business life; and, inevitably, many of this respected executive's colleagues think of his horses as a "nice hobby."

Virtually every minute in the life of this man is consumed by his desire to create beauty and laughter. And the quality that makes him so enthusiastic, and makes his associates love him so devotedly, has to do with the great range of his varied talents and interests, including both music and art. His wife was once asked whether her husband and sons, all of whom have won nearly every jumping competition they ever entered, were concerned mainly with horses because they had spent so many hours in the saddle. The reply was simply, "A *real* horseman can't help but have a myriad of other talents."

The wife's reasoning? Since a love for horses and the skill to train them require a knowledge of psychology—to understand the mind of a sensitive living creature—and a great empathy for the emotions of others, an experienced equestrian naturally knows how to interact with people and can sail through life in all its many aspects. Or, to put it a little differently, when a person is able to keep his mind fresh and alert to new sensitivity on the part of a horse, he inevitably seeks other diverting, mind-stretching activity to stimulate him to new ideas and challenges.

Dedicated to the development of human potential and the heightening of his horsemanship students' athletic and mental abilities, this man can be called the actualizer as well as the actualized. His motive lies, not in producing winners so that he will gain a better reputation as an instructor, but in showing each pupil how to test himself, his self-discipline, and his ability to overcome fear. After falling, or before facing large crowds during competition, a new rider can become scared, and the cop-out has always been: "I hate that horse." Or: "I didn't really want to learn anyway." But this born actualizer will have none of that!

A taskmaster, this man has established a humorous rapport in his stable. But, when he makes a request, he is obeyed as though he had given an order. Instead of demanding or telling people, he asks and expects quality performance. As a consequence, the final result is winning students and a professional stable.

In Love with Life

What, you may ask, makes this man so obviously fulfilled? A number of clearly relevant factors may be summed up here:

- His multifaceted life.
- His genuine interest in people.
- His intense desire to create beauty with his animals and in his music and art.
- His ability to see humor in every situation.
- His continuing appetite for reading.
- His high expectations in every dimension of living.
- His rich spiritual life—one of *caring, expecting,* and *becoming.*

Not only is this man a complete equestrian success, but he is considered Mr. Horseman by many people in the American horse world. From the age of 20 he began to consume volume after volume on horsemanship while also developing his musical talents and building his manufacturing company. By refusing to fall into easy cynicism or brood over the occasional failure, his own or others', he has surrounded himself with an aura of laughter which makes the hard work he exacts almost easy. Yet he is uncompromising with his pupils.

After a two-hour session on horseback in the hot mid-afternoon summer sun, one member of a group remarked, "I'll always remember these workouts. They're the kind you think will never end, but the kind you look back on—knowing darn well that you learned a lot. I guess that's what makes us all love the guy so much."

Perhaps that is, in part, the essence of the man's success. For he has spent the major part of his life giving of self.

Though renowned in his field, he cares enough to encourage others. Once he spent two days riding in a dressage clinic given by a young woman and listening to her teach. He did not criticize her, although her knowledge and skill were miniscule when compared to his own. Instead, he posed as a student and asked questions which would move the lessons along more smoothly, helping the teacher learn at the same time.

Also, this man disciplines his own mind even more strongly than those of his students. He has fallen, gotten up again, and then taken another and yet another fall so that his dream—including an indoor riding hall, a beautiful barn, and a deserved reputation for horsemanship based firmly on his own ability—would become a reality. All this took him nearly 40 years. Now, instead of griping and limping, at 65 he looks 50 and acts as young as the happiest child. In love with his wife, his work, and especially life, he has had goals, demanded hard work of himself, met his personal commitments, and found a life style challenging enough for any man.

When asked how old he expects to live to be, he says with a twinkle, "Ask me when I reach middle age!" We suspect he'd agree with these words of Edwin Markham:

> Ah, great it is to believe the dream
> As we stand in youth by the starry stream;
> But a greater thing is to fight life through,
> And say at the end, "The Dream is true!" [5]

We Are All Becoming . . .

What are we becoming? Perhaps there is no more important question for the manager in any enterprise—

whether business, school, or home—to ask himself. It is his example which will speak more loudly than his words. It is his expectations of self which will determine his expectations of his job, his subordinates, his peers, and those executives in higher positions. It is his trust in himself which will determine how much he trusts others. It is his love for self which will determine his love for others. In short, it is his input into life as a whole person which will determine the output of that total life of which his managerial job is a crucial part—but only a part.

The editors of *Perceiving, Behaving, Becoming*, published by the National Education Association, put it this way:

> The development of adequate persons who see themselves in the process of becoming seems to hold significant promise for the future. The person who sees this process is open to change and trusts his impulses and values as guides for behavior in new circumstances. Such persons are probably most likely to adapt and survive as the environment changes. Such persons will be able to create ways to meet new conditions. We cannot predict the world of 2015 when today's kindergartners will be dealing with a very different world of ideas, people and processes. We cannot know which bits of present information will be needed in that world. We can be very certain, however, that providing schools which facilitate the development of persons with adequate, fully functioning personalities is the best way to contribute some degree of stability to an uncertain future. The person who has a positive view of self, who is open to experience, who is creative, who is trustworthy and responsible, who has values, who is well informed, and who is aware that he is in the process of becoming is the person most able to survive and deal with the future. What is more, he will do a better job for the rest of us.[6]

This kind of person, leading what we hope will become *a massive revolutionary renewal of confidence,* will face obstacles and difficulties and will encounter creative opportunities which can make the other revolutions of history mere peristaltic tremors.

If you share our belief that man is a unique and potentially splendid creation of a living God; if you believe with us that man is much more than some kind of soulless animal, we challenge you to storm the ramparts of today's dissension-torn world. There is an aching need for new thinking which will glorify rather than denigrate human life. The options are clearly etched, and *you* have the precious freedom to choose.

What are *you* becoming?

Take the Time

An anonymous poet has said.

> He hadn't time to pen a note,
> He hadn't time to cast a vote.
> He hadn't time to sing a song,
> He hadn't time to right a wrong.
> He hadn't time to love or give,
> He hadn't time to really live.
> From now on he'll have time on end—
> He died today, my "busy" friend.

The time is NOW! And we—two generations, father and daughter—think that's great. Any challenges?

REFERENCES

1. Lawrence Lessing, "The Senseless War on Science," *Fortune* (March 1971).
2. Eric Hoffer, "Thoughts of Eric Hoffer . . . ," *The New York Times,* April 25, 1971, © 1971 by The New York Times Company. Reprinted by permission.
3. Richard L. Kattel, "The New Youth Movement." Reprinted by special permission from DUN's, August 1971. Copyright, 1971, Dun & Bradstreet Publications Corp.
4. Charles Reich, *The Greening of America* (New York: Random House, 1970), p. 75.
5. Edwin Markham, "The Dream," in *One Thousand Quotable Poems,* edited by Thomas Clark (New York: Clark & Co., 1937).
6. Association for Supervision and Curriculum Development, *Perceiving, Behaving, Becoming: A New Focus for Education.* 1962 Yearbook. Arthur W. Combs, chairman. Washington, D.C.: the Association, 1962. Chapter 15, p. 253.

Appendix A
Reply to Darkness

THE following poem is written in the idiom of the rock opera *Jesus Christ, Superstar* and was intended as a relevant Christian "secularistic" response to what was felt to be the challenge inherent in the original lines.

Reply to Darkness
by Gail Batten

Hey there, Savior Jesus Christ,
What is it made you sacrifice?
That life we value You threw out.
But people didn't really shout.
They put You down—called You no king,
Said that Your life meant not a thing.
We still live now in misery and wallow in our sin.

Oh, Jesus Christ, you crazy man . . .
What made You rise to live again?
Can You still love these lives we lead
Of pain and hate and greed?

Or is there something we don't know,
A fire that sets Your soul aglow?

Oh, come on, Jesus . . . You aren't king.
Where's that immortal life You bring?
If You're so great then tell us how
To find the answers to love—right now.

O.K., you call me Superstar. . . .
I don't get drunk or go too far.
But do I ever put you down
For taking time to mess around?
I don't condone the narrow life
All filled with toil and fear and strife.
My task on earth's no simple one,
To show you God can be great fun.

I know you laugh—you play it cool
And think me one gigantic fool.
But do you really understand
What it's like at God's right hand?
Come on, you say, "Why should we pray?
Walk piously around all day?"
I fear you all don't really see
That gift God gave to you and me.
You've all been taught the Savior Man
Was words and love—a gentle lamb.

You're too hung up on all your needs
To see I was a man of deeds.
I roared with laughter, partied after,
For humor and jokes there was no one faster.
Too bad all my Biblical verse
Is destined to an endless curse . . . of misunderstanding.

We all had fun, the Twelve and I.
Not drugs—but love. We soon got high.
We talked with God—and loved ourselves
And didn't live in little hells.
I hope you hear now what I say,
Because I live with you today.

Yes, Jesus Christ, that fabled Man,
Dwells here on earth in every land.
In heart and mind—new peace you'll find,
If you see that Christ was not *just* kind!
But, full of vital energy,
He lives and loves life passionately.
And with Christ's scarifice of self
He helps to save somebody else,
By bringing facts of life to you,
By showing you that God means Truth.

He gave his soul, came back from Hell,
Helped us survive our smothered shell.
He hopes to make us plainly choose
God above drugs and excessive booze.
Sure, you can still have sinful times
If God turns out to be all lies.
But try Christ first—give Him a chance
And know that life will be enhanced.

Appendix B   The Young Manager/Leader of Tomorrow

THE two profiles which follow should in no way be construed as limited to the manager or leader in the world of business and industry. Rather, they are intended—as is this entire book—for the present or potential leader in any facet of the broad spectrum of American endeavor. We include here the professions, the churches, government, labor, the home, our educational institutions—wherever human talent and experience are applied to "getting things done through people."

Profile
by Gail Batten

It's almost impossible to devise a profile of tomorrow's manager, because he isn't going to be able to sit down and tick off what causes he believes in, what procedures he must follow, or which authors he is to quote and hold sacred. But, in order to survive in tomorrow's business world, the new manager and leader must be

1. Goal-oriented, action-centered.
2. Of no particular "generation."
3. More transglobal in thought than trans-American.
4. Ready to assume total responsibility at all times.
5. Able to delegate jobs and responsibilities.
6. Able to demand performance because workers respect their manager, not fear him or fear losing a job.
7. Capable of fusing the ideas and policies of various individuals into corporate practices.
8. Willing to forget dogmatism and accept flexibility.
9. Educated, with a workable set of ideas and the ability to understand the ideas of others.
10. Widely read; continually searching for new, provocative ideas to stimulate and challenge himself and his workers.
11. Able to utilize individual differences within his organization.
12. Able to integrate the dynamics of life outside the organizational world so as to combine empathy with pragmatic practice.

Tomorrow's manager must like himself enough to keep his mind open continually to the sensitivity of people and the world surrounding him. In this way his organization will maintain an atmosphere of creativity, vitality, and credibility.

Profile
by Joe Batten

1. The young manager/leader's educational preparation tomorrow will be multidisciplinary.

2. His academic credentials may well be the product of new forms of education whose modular dimensions are now shaping. For instance, the video possibilities of innovative new forms of home study are distinctly promising.

3. He may be, according to James W. McSwiney, president of the Mead Corporation, "more concerned with private, personal self-fulfillment than with corporate efficiency."

4. The term "quality" and what it connotes will be more dominant in his vocabulary and actions than "quantity."

5. He will, in general, not allow himself to become walled within an occupational posture which seems to require protracted defensive behavior.

6. He will be productivity-oriented, but will see productivity in four dimensions: economic, social, political, spiritual.

7. He will see management as an art, not a science, and will seek to understand and utilize all the relevant tools and resources of science. Art is at the summit of man's experience; science can provide the paths, the vehicles, and some of the fuel to get there.

8. He will be mentally flexible and will constantly strive to maintain and gain new flexibility.

9. He will believe and understand that fully functioning people are people with strong values, beliefs, and convictions.

10. He will not be content with inadequate patchwork methods of teaching the full meaning of the profit motive to all employees, but will utilize the bud-

ding excellence implicit in audio-video technology and curriculum preparation.

11. He will be in a perpetual state of flow, of process. He will feel and exemplify a high level of trust and creativity.

12. He will waste little time on dialogue or the disputation of despair. He will be too busy *building*.

13. He will believe in and practice the tough-minded administrative process known as accountability. He will believe that all the resources of the organization must be held accountable for making a genuine contribution to the overall results, and he will implement managemental breakthroughs and human insights which will increasingly base rewards on contribution. Outdated and superficial indices —old school ties, good looks, color, race, creed, "niceness"—will be relatively meaningless. He will be much more concerned with *what the person is* and *what he gets done*.

14. He will be a product of management training that has stressed understanding others rather than understanding *about* others. He will be more successful at this than his predecessors because he will possess *better insight into himself*.